DINAH'S REBELLION:
A BIBLICAL PARABLE FOR OUR TIME

DINAH'S REBELLION:
A BIBLICAL PARABLE
FOR OUR TIME

Ita Sheres

CROSSROAD • NEW YORK

To my mother, Ahuva,
may she rest in peace.

The Crossroad Publishing Company
370 Lexington Avenue
New York, NY 10017

Printed in the United States of America

Library of Congress Cataloging in Publication Data

Sheres, Ita.
  Dinah's rebellion : a biblical parable for our time / by Ita
Sheres.
      p.   cm.
  Includes bibliographical references.
  ISBN 0-8245-1014-3
  1. Dinah (Biblical character).   2. Women in the Bible. I. Title.
BS580.D55S53   1990
222'.11092--dc20   90-33671
                                                          CIP

CONTENTS

ACKNOWLEDGMENTS

I wish to thank Professor Max Ticktin of George Washington University for his suggestions and comments on the early drafts of this study; Professor Arthur Springer was similarly helpful. Special thanks go to Professor David Noel Freedman, who made very insightful comments and who maintained that indeed Dinah was a very important woman.

FOREWORD

This book by Ita Sheres is a stimulating and provocative study of a well-known story in the book of Genesis: the rape of Dinah. Dr. Sheres examines the narrative in Genesis 34 from a literary-critical and feminist perspective, showing how what has been left out is often as important as what has been included in the account. She focuses attention on unusual and distinctive features of the story, in particular the "silence" of Dinah, who has no voice in the story at all, or in the whole book of Genesis.

While Dr. Sheres concentrates on two versions of the narrative— that of the author, presumably the scholarly construct "J," and that of the redactor, "R"—and shows how each has shaped or positioned it to convey an important male-oriented message, she also speculates in a creative fashion about a supposed original tale underlying the present biblical account, in which Dinah plays a much more substantive role in the community and in which no rape occurs. To round off this modernist approach Dr. Sheres brings the story into the contemporary scene of Israeli-Palestinian confrontation and offers her own redaction, midrash, and adaptation in analyzing and evaluating the current struggle between Palestinians and Israelis for possession and occupation of the biblical heartland, the scene of the original collision and conflict between the sons of Jacob and the Hivites (Horites) in the region of ancient Shechem (modern Nablus).

DAVID NOEL FREEDMAN
University of Michigan, Ann Arbor
University of California, San Diego

INTRODUCTION

The Text of Genesis 34

A N D   D I N A H, the daughter of Leah that she bore to Jacob, went out to see among the daughters of the land. And Shechem the son of Hamor, the Hivite prince of the land, saw her and took her and lay with her and tortured her. And his soul cleaved to Dinah the daughter of Jacob, and he loved the girl and he spoke to the girl's heart. And Shechem told his father Hamor, "Take this child for me as a wife." And Jacob heard that he had defiled Dinah his daughter; and his sons were with his cattle in the field; and Jacob was silent until they returned. And Hamor, the father of Shechem, went out to Jacob to speak with him. And the sons of Jacob came back from the field as soon as they heard; and they were grieved and very angry, because it was an outrage in Israel to lie with the daughter of Jacob, something which was not done. And Hamor spoke to them saying, "Shechem my son, his soul desires your daughter; give her to him as a wife, and you can marry among us, you may give your daughters to us and take our daughters; and settle with us and the land will be yours, settle and trade within it and acquire it." And Shechem said to her father and her brothers, "Please [literally, "I wish to satisfy you"], I will give you anything that you say, increase as much as you want the dowry and the gifts; I will give whatever you say, and let me have the girl for a wife." And the sons of Jacob answered Shechem deceptively, and they were discussing the fact that he had defiled Dinah their sister. And they said to them, "We cannot do such a thing as giving our sister to a man who has his foreskin, because it is shameful to us. But we will be willing to accommodate you if you will be like us, that is, circumcise all of your males; and we will give you our daughters and will take your

1

daughters and settle with you and we will be one people. And if you
will not listen to us with regard to circumcision, we will take our
daughter and walk away." And their words were fair in the eyes of
Hamor and in the eyes of Shechem, the son of Hamor. And the boy
did not lose time to do the thing because he wanted the daughter
of Jacob; and he was the most respected in the house of his father.
And Hamor and his son Shechem came to the gate of their city and
they talked to the people of their city saying, "These people are
forthright with us and they [wish to] settle in the land and do
commerce within it; and the land has plenty of space, and we can
take their daughters as wives and give them our daughters. But
there is this condition that these people require of us so that they
will settle with us and be one people, namely, that all our males be
circumcised just like they are circumcised. Their cattle and possessions and all their animals are ours, if only we agree, and they will
settle with us." And they listened to Hamor and to Shechem his son,
all those who went out to the city's gate, and they circumcised all
the males of all those who went out to the city gate. And it came to
pass that on the third day, when they were aching, and the two sons
of Jacob, Simeon and Levi, the brothers of Dinah, took their sword
and they came upon the town while it was safe [the Shechemites
thought they were safe] and they killed all the males. And Hamor
and Shechem his son they killed by the sword; and they took Dinah
out of the house of Shechem and they went out. The sons of Jacob
came upon the dead and they looted the city that had defiled their
sister. They took their flocks and cattle and asses that were in the
city and in their field; and all their possessions, and children and
wives they took captive, and they looted everything that was in the
house. And Jacob said to Simeon and Levi, "You have brought ill
repute on me so that I will be obnoxious to the settlers of the land,
the Canaanites and the Perizzites; and I am few in numbers so that
they can now congregate on me and defeat me and destroy me and
my house." And they said, "Will our full sister be treated like a
whore?"

The Dinah Narrative

The core of this study is the story of Dinah, the daughter of Jacob
and Leah and the sister of Simeon and Levi. She is here viewed as

a woman who was like other women in Genesis as well as very different from them. This examination focuses on the connection between the redactors of Genesis — who ultimately assisted in defining the terms of Jewish survival after the destruction of the First Hebrew Commonwealth in 586 B.C.E., and who were influenced by their own political experiences in exile — and Dinah. It was the redactors who put the final stamp on the portrait of Dinah as well as on those of all the other men and women in the text; and the specific manner in which Dinah appears in the text is due mainly to their ideological convictions. The redactors by and large projected an unfavorable attitude to women because of the particular way they viewed their own universe. Thus, for example, they included in the text instances of violence toward women not only because these were real but mainly because it suited their purpose of advocating a distinctly ideological position which ultimately was linked to women, violence, and the world at large.

The story of Dinah is both physically and mentally cruel; it starts out innocently enough by stating that Dinah went out "to see the daughters of the land." (Presumably that phrase indicates an attempt on her part to socialize with Canaanite women because the "land" under consideration indeed is Canaan.) But Dinah meets with disaster when Shechem, a Hivite nāśí' (privileged person), rapes her; curiously, though, he then falls in love with her and arranges for a traditional courtship. This involves also Shechem's father, who in turn approaches the family of the bride-to-be with a matrimonial offer. Jacob, Dinah's father, hears about the rape but remains silent. When Dinah's brothers (particularly Simeon and Levi and not Judah and Reuben who had different territorial interests; Reuben's land was east of the Jordan, while Judah's territory was far to the south of Shechem) are informed about the abominable action of Shechem, they are quite disturbed. Nonetheless, both Shechem's family and Jacob's family do get together in order to discuss the terms of the betrothal. The Hivites seem to have a sweeping view of the outcome of a potential marriage between Shechem and Dinah, and they offer Jacob and his sons environmental as well as commercial integration. The brothers, who are still indignant about Shechem's action, are not favorably disposed. In a devious maneuver they inform the Hivites that their sister's marriage to Shechem is now contingent on the whole Hivite tribe's

acceptance of the rite of circumcision, which, so the brothers maintain, will cleanse and properly prepare the Hivites to enter into a
marriage contract with the Hebrew family. The brothers proclaim
that the tradition of their ancestors (circumcision of the males) must
be closely followed before any marriage can take place. The Hivites
leave the bargaining table and move on to discuss the issue with
their compatriots, who, because of the social position of Shechem's
family, agree to the Jacobites' terms and consequently are circumcised. Simeon and Levi descend on the tribe, on the third day "while
the Hivites were still in pain" and immobile, and slaughter all the
males. The women, children, and animals are taken as booty, and
Dinah is seized from Shechem's house. When Jacob hears what his
sons have done, he is furious because he is convinced that it will be
impossible for him to live peacefully and trade in that area. When
he admonishes his sons accordingly, they respond: "Will our sister
be treated like a whore?"

From a purely literary perspective, the story is about a woman
who left her father's house and met with disaster. Although the text
never refers to Shechem's act as "rape," it does use linguistic "signs"
which indicate that a violent sexual act took place. Paradoxically,
after the implied rape occurred, the villain fell in love with the
object of his villainy and was ready to marry her. Ironically,
Shechem's wish to wed Dinah falls precisely within the parameters
of biblical law, which prescribes marriage as well as a substantial
mōhar[1] for a man who violates a virgin (Exod 22:15–16). Deutero-
nomic law is even stricter and demands that the offender "give the
father of the maiden fifty silver and she will be his because he
tortured her. (The text uses the verb *'nh*, which is the same verb as
that used in the Dinah narrative.) He will not be able to divorce her
all of his days (life)" (22:29). It seems that from the beginning, the
narrators prepare us for a story filled with paradoxes, contradic-
tions, and ironies. These, in turn, alert the reader to literary
tensions and ambiguities, but they also prepare us for a message
that does not remain within the realm of literature alone.

Since there is no doubt about the redactive nature of the story (as
I will attempt to show), it is important to examine the redaction
along with the intent of the redactors. Intent can be shown by the
final impact that the story had on those who were a part of it as well
as those who read and evaluated it. In other words, like any other

work of art, the Dinah narrative has an author (or, authors) who operate(s) from within a certain framework as well as an audience who responds to the author's creation. However, because of the complex nature of Genesis, specifically in the realm of editing and redacting, it is also the task of this probe to determine whether there was another Dinah story that the redactors chose to change, ignore, or cut for reasons that were not just literary. I will attempt to show, structurally, politically, and psychologically, that indeed the redactors had access to a core rape story that involved a sister and avenging brother(s). Additionally, since there are other biblical stories linking circumcision (as a ploy and not as a ritual demand) with death and destruction, they will have to be more closely looked into so as to determine not only the literary tradition that the redactors followed but the possible political agenda that they pursued. In all of the above incidents, the role (or, non-role) of women and strangers will be underscored.

The main argument of this book is that, from the redactors' vantage point, the story of Dinah, while intrinsically about a sister who was violated by a strange man — and in that sense is not very different from other stories in other traditions about violated and abused women — undertakes to draw the line between an individual's moral behavior and his/her social and political commitments. The story's ultimate premise lies in the redactors' belief that there is a deep link between moral behavior, political commitment, and the individual's position in the universe.

It should be noted from the outset that the other story linked with rape, Amnon's rape of Tamar in 2 Samuel 16, has an overwhelming amount of political intrigue, all of which relates to King David's court. In yet another story, tied with circumcision as a ruse (1 Sam 18:25–30), there is no escaping the political agenda of Saul against David. Similarly, at the heart of the Dinah narrative there is an extended discussion between the Hebrews and the Hivites about commerce and intertribal relations, about political land settlements and intermarriage. Indeed, if one were to attempt to place the story in an earlier age than the sixth century B.C.E. and associate its contents with another people — the Hurrians (not Hivites), who prospered in Palestine in the fifteenth century B.C.E.[2] — then it is nothing but a story about some Hebrews who struggle to find legal residence in a territory that happens to be occupied by another tribe. Further, even in the redacted version of the story, the text uses symbols pertinent to the realm of covenantal promises, and these promises are the tale's chief literary vehicles. But, in the biblical landscape, covenantal promises are not only indicative of the Divine's viable presence in history; rather, they are concrete examples of human politics particularly in the sphere of land possession. Hence, the historical essence of the story is political and land-oriented. In other words, the redacted tale of Dinah evolves around the Hebrews' territorial needs, which achieved a certain peak during the reign of David and Solomon and which became even more pronounced after the fall of Jerusalem in the wake of the Babylonian conquest in 586 B.C.E.

It is no coincidence that scholars and commentators rightly claim that Hebraic historiography originated during the days of the monarchy or, at the very latest, at the end of the First Commonwealth, when that monarchy drew to a close. The book of Genesis, which is not necessarily about Hebrew kings and monarchs, is crucial to the development of that history; and in some instances, Genesis alludes overtly to events that were closely related to monarchic times.[3]

In the context of politics, the Jacob family, within which Dinah operates, is presented as looking for an appropriate settlement in Canaan, and, according to at least one approach to the text, the story of Dinah is nothing but an explanation for the special position of the tribes of Simeon and Levi in later Israelite history. More concretely, some commentators claim that the Dinah tale elaborates on a major rift between some Canaanite settlers and the Israelites on the latter's way to political entrenchment in Canaan.[4] In this context, it is generally agreed that the story points to a decline in fortunes for Simeon and Levi, whose frustrations and anger are clearly visible in the tale itself.

If examined structurally, the narrative equips Dinah with some power. In fact, the opening verse of the chapter leads one to believe that the rest of the story is about Dinah. In a purely literary environment, Dinah's action, even if it is ultimately condemned, leads one to assume that she will be provided with a voice that will further elucidate her action. As her "going out" signifies, this story belongs to a whole genre of accounts dealing with women (as well as men) who were on the way to self-discovery. A gnostic might have called

Dinah's "outing" a bold act that implied individuality and purpose, since she was on her way out of the house of Jacob and in the direction of "the women of the land."[5] Unfortunately for her, the gnostic aspect of her act was transformed into an institutional response, and she had to return home, a sign of order, conservatism, and presumably stability. Moreover, the price that Dinah had to pay for attempting to break away from tradition was a loss of voice. There are other women in Genesis who have distinct personalities, assume obvious actions, and have clear voices, but Dinah is not one of them, as we will see.

One of the main reasons for the woman's loss of personal traits and characteristics is the deliberate political message of the tale. When a story has political ramifications and purports to convey a theme that is overwhelmingly territorial, the woman's voice falters. Part of the reason for the deemphasis of women's roles in the politics of Genesis is that the book is indeed patriarchal and therefore deliberately manipulated. The patriarchal imperative appropriates clear realms for women and men; women belong in an a-political domain, and men engender a tremendous amount of power and control from political maneuvers. More important, the males in the Genesis narratives are heavily involved in transforming basic values —Mesopotamian (their presumed point of embarkation) or otherwise—which seemed to have originated from a more matriarchally centered society. Their main weapons of cultural and social transformation were land and male descendants. The women, who could have had political roles—as priestesses, for example—were restricted from significant participation in any public social and political service and had to be limited to strictly "biological" functions which demanded that they remain within the home. In order to emphasize the loss of womanly political operation, some of the major social and religious rituals and ceremonies in the biblical stories were reconstructed so as to highlight the role of men. For example, the celebration of the Sabbath, which originally was associated with the Babylonian Shapattu and was celebrated once a month on the day of the full moon (an echo of goddess worship and fertility cults),[6] was transformed by the Hebrews into a weekly, seventh-day celebration related to the Yahwistic covenant. The Hebrew Sabbath celebrated, on the one hand, the orderly creation of the world by a male deity and, on the other hand, the Hebrews' deliverance from Egypt. That event too was associated with Yahweh's power and covenantal promise to the patriarchs. It should be noted here that the events of the exodus too are filled with clear instances of woman's power which are yet to be fully unraveled and explicated.[7] Another institution, circumcision, was referred to as the "sign" of the covenant. It was totally transformed for ideological reasons and emphasized the role differences of men and women. This will be dealt with at length further on.

Dinah's story ultimately provides the political framework for what develops in Jewish history as a rigid ideology of land and people. Within that ideology, women were placed where they "belonged," namely, inside their father's (and/or brothers') house. So it was that from the redactors' perspective, the events in the tale were occurrences that befell the woman Dinah and her rapist, because of a fundamental ideological breach manifested in the confrontation between the Hebrew woman and the Hivite prince. Indeed, Dinah was portrayed first of all as a victim; but she was also a responsible party in the crime because she undertook the forbidden (by the redactors) act of "going out to see the women of the land."

It is suggested here that the Dinah narrative demonstrates the impact of what became a stern nationalistic agenda that sometimes placed land and possessions (two major ingredients of Yahweh's covenant with the patriarchs) above universal and humanistic values. By contrast, it is suggested that even though the woman of the story is abused and maligned, she is one of the only participants who is ready to go forth with a compassionate agenda of inclusion and sharing. Similarly, the women of the two other stories that deal with rape and circumcision, Tamar and Michal, are presented as wise, compassionate, and loving while their male counterparts wreak havoc and destruction.

Jewish Nationalism

The nationalistic aspirations of the Jews are very closely related to a great event in their history—the deliverance from Egyptian bondage. It was at Sinai that the Hebrews were approached by an all-powerful God and committed themselves to "a life of dialogue." "But," argues Martin Buber, "it required a great inner transformation to make them into a nation. In the course of this inner change, the concept of the government of God took on a political form . . . the kingdom as the representative of God."[8] Buber goes on to say that the uniqueness of Jewish nationalism lies in its peculiar links to the concept of a "community of faith" without which it (nationalism) can quickly deteriorate into "an end in itself" where there is no room "for supernational ethical demands." In that case, says Buber, "legitimate nationalism" will be supplanted by "arbitrary nationalism." Buber's fear for those who aspire to Jewish nationalism is that they will proclaim "the nation as an end in itself" and that "formal nationalism" will ultimately sanction a group egoism that disclaims responsibility."[9] That responsibility, in Buber's mind, is first and foremost toward "the other," who is both different from the "I" and like the "I." "The other becomes present, not merely in the imagination or feeling, but in the depths of one's substance, so that one experiences the mystery of the other being in the mystery of one's own."[10] The deep concern of Buber (and others who share his convictions) is that a unique national destiny can deteriorate into a nationalistic superiority that has no room for anyone who is out of the rigidly defined ideological line. Buber maintains that the "will" of the Jewish people is to fulfill the truth of God, and for that purpose they must build a social pattern that will embrace all facets of existence, "from the pattern of family, neighborhood and settlement to that of the whole community. For it is no real community if it is not composed of real families and real neighborhoods and real settlements, and it is not a real nation if it does not maintain its truthfulness in true relations as well, the relationships of a fruitful and creative peace with its neighbors."[11] The emphasis on "family, neighborhood, and community" echoes Buber's strong belief in the viability of an intimate framework that allows for a close, profound interplay between the various members of a given community. Buber is also concerned about the "true" and the "real," which further points to his regard for "the other" as much as for the "I." Truth can emerge only within a fully egalitarian structure, and the real is manifested in the dialogical posture which allows all members of the community to deliberate and define their positions and concerns.

In attempting to apply these reservations about nationalism, we will try to read the story of Dinah as a parable where the "I" of the family of Jacob/Israel meets "the other" of the clan of the Hivites with disastrous results. Not only does the confrontation between the two groups bring out the worst in the brothers of the woman; it also indicts the sister (who did attempt to approach the Hivites from an I-Thou position), whose ill-fated adventure stigmatized her for the rest of her life. The reading will also demonstrate that within the Jacob family there was a deep split between the patriarch and his sons as well as between the father and the daughter, which further contributed to the basic posture of alienation and distrust that governs the whole affair. Dinah is silenced because of her family standing, which was basically very weak, as well as because of the social position that she took. The woman's search for the Canaanites and her willingness to visit with them were contrary to the apartness of the redactors, who had to end her inclusive attempts as early as possible.

The redactive silence of Dinah is the most powerful weapon used in the text to undermine the woman's political attitude. Her victimization in the story is at the hand of Shechem, the Hivite, but really she is exploited by the hand of the redactors. Her "redemption" is at the hands of her brothers. But, in one of the many ironic twists of the story, there is another victim, namely, the whole Hivite tribe, which was not involved in the initial rape and which had to undergo mutilation and death. The Hivites who perish, like Dinah, are also silent; they are ultimately the victims of a fanatic ideology that demands territory even at the price of human life and dignity.

If we were to use contemporary political, Middle Eastern terms of discourse, we might liken the brothers' confrontation with the Hivites to Rabbi Meir Kahane's approach to the question of the Palestinians in the occupied territories. Kahane, who likes to quote the Deuteronomists, is nothing but an extreme manifestation of the rejection of the Buberian political world view. His interpretation of the Sinaitic legacy stands diametrically opposed to that of Buber. Kahane's advocacy of violence and racism while serving the cause of "I-It" also undermines in the most profound way Buber's position that "the world of relation," which is the authentic sphere of the I-Thou, is so seriously damaged when confronted with racism and intolerance that it might be irreparably doomed. More than that, the utter alienation of Kahane's statement— "the Arab in Israel will never be as equal as the Jew"[12]—is a repetition of the act of Cain against his brother, which in Buber's mind was the result of Cain's refusal to face himself before facing his brother — thus, the compulsion to murder, separate, and isolate. The total involvement of the "I" with himself is delivering Cain to his "desires." The murderer lacks "self-relationship," which is, in turn, mirrored in his inability to have a "relationship" with his brother. Indeed, Kahane's statement about the basic inequality of the Arab is a cruel manifestation of Cain's inability to handle dialogue with his brother on any level and particularly "when they were in the field" (Gen 4:8), where the text breaks down completely and the expected verbal exchange between Cain and Abel never takes place. Tragically, however, the murder of Abel occurs in that same "field."

By comparison, Dinah's initial attitude to the Hivites is indeed Buberian, but her ultimate silence is echoed in the current Israeli silence of a great majority of men and women who do wish to engage in a dialogue with the Palestinians. The contemporary equivalents of the sixth-century redactors are also motivated by a particular understanding of Jewish history which is painful and traumatic. Indeed, the impact of the Hitlerian *shoah* (holocaust) cannot be overlooked in any discussion of Jewish nationalism and Zionism, just as it is impossible to assess the contribution of the biblical redactors without accounting for their traumatic experiences associated with the imperial Babylonian takeover of the kingdom of Judah. Moreover, the trauma experienced and expressed by both groups of people in the ancient world as well as now is mainly attributed to an exilic condition that did not foster nationalism. The redactors operated in Babylonia, articulating a national ideology from within a typically non-national framework. Actually, it has already been suggested that they were particularly wary of the disaster of 722, which wiped out ten Hebrew tribes, who were totally assimilated into the Assyrian environment.[13] The modern Zionists were prompted into heightened activity as a result of the Dreyfus affair in France at the end of the nineteenth century, as well as after the Second World War, when Hitler's atrocities became widely known. In fact, a strong argument can be made about current Israeli politics, which is still dominated by a group of people (mostly men) who have been under the influence of the *shoah* all of their lives. The redactors too, if not themselves exiles from Jerusalem, were influenced by the Babylonian destruction and ultimately went on to articulate a Zionist-type ideology, maintaining in effect that in order to live a complete Jewish life a Jew must return to a Jewish homeland, which is the land that Yahweh promised to the Hebrew patriarchs. It is interesting to point out that both of these "Zionist" articulators were operating from without "the holy land" even though the main focus of their ideological speculations was Canaan/Israel/Judea. Both of these groups of people were well educated, and if they were not themselves assimilated into the environment, then they clearly had the capability of rationalizing the impact of assimilation. The redactors who utilized religious terminology professed that the land given to the Hebrews belonged to Yahweh, the creator of the whole cosmos. He chose to give Canaan to his people as an act of grace, and they have to live within its confines and according to his rules and laws. The main asset missing from the covenantal arrangement between God and his people is compromise, without which the more extreme, fanatical elements ultimately begin to flourish. Additionally, the idea of the covenant gives rise to a series of attitudes on the part of those who perceive themselves as "chosen" and "special." Although choice can connote extraordinary opportunities, it is also a harbinger of rigidity, stiffness, and isolationism. The description of Israel as a "people who dwells all to itself" (*lĕbādād,* "all alone") (Num 23:9) is accurate and acute because in its more extreme moments it becomes a desperate condition that has the potential of outrage leading to violence. The chosen person walks the thin line of elation on the one hand and anger on the other. Since the chosen people are conceptually God's representatives on earth, it is no accident that Yahweh loves Israel, but he is also jealous of Israel's defections and disloyalties. He thus is compelled to punish them whenever they betray him. The tension between God's expectations and the nation's conduct leads sometimes to excessive actions that can be detrimental to other people's lives. For example, the emphasis on the special land given to Abraham and future generations, and its tie with the "holy nation," led ultimately to repulsive behavior toward the inhabitants of Canaan, who, for the Hebrews, became the emblems of a corrupt community that must be annihilated.

It is not my intent here to analyze fully the connection between land possession, nationalism, and the role of women, but a general statement to that effect is in order.

There is no question about the inherent dangers of correlating or objectifying people—male or female—with certain features of the landscape. The most universal association of this kind juxtaposes the land with women. In that context, the latter are referred to as closely linked with the earth because of their childbearing capacities; they are thus also more "earth"-prone as opposed to mind- or sensibility-prone. If one were to review the myriad biblical references to the land ('ereṣ), one would conclude that the noun used is deliberately feminine.[14] From its very beginning, the idea of settling and later on conquering the land, is androcentric and carefully prepares us for a domination that could be transformed into the realm of interpersonal and intersexual relations as well. Among the many references to Canaan as the land of milk and honey (as well as various other expressions that convey the idea of plenitude), time and again the writers describe the territory as "a good and wide land" (Exod 3:8) or "a land that Yahweh your God is seeking" (Deut 11:12). The imagery invoked conveys the idea of courtship, and the male deity is involved in pursuing the land that is furnished for the people. As the association of land and women develops in the text, it appears to be related to cleanness and holiness and ultimately to sexual and moral perversion. The Priestly code focuses on cleanliness and warns that if "the land is polluted, I [God] will visit her sin upon her and I will cause her [the land] to vomit her settlers" (Lev 18:25). The links between land fecundity and women's fertility are stressed time and again, and the most terrifying punishment visited upon the Hebrews is indeed expressed as total sterility—of the land as well as of the people (particularly, women).[15] The classical prophets, more than anyone else in the Hebraic tradition, expressed their outrage about the people's immorality by using the land–woman device: "You have polluted the land with your whorish depravity" (Jer 3:2b); "You are an impure land with no rain on a day of rage" (Ezek 22:24). The whole of Hosea is dedicated to an exploration of the many connections between landscape (trees and mountains) and women's depravity (Baal worship). The prophets' tone and attitude toward women is negative; indeed, it is at times so venomous that some scholars have suggested that the prophets were misogynists.[16] Whether the source of the prophets' misogynism was personal or not is hard to determine, but it was adopted by the redactors who used it in their strategy to divest women of any power. Misogynism was accompanied by objectification, which made it easier to view women as commodities that function for a particular purpose. The redactors thus elaborated on the land-scape–sexual connection because it enabled them to separate women from their men by converting them into sexual vessels totally dependent on the land for their fertility, which, in turn, marked their social standing. The ingenious aspect of the land–woman metaphor is particularly striking when placed within the framework of reward and punishment: namely, if the people are "good" they are rewarded with "rains" that replenish the land; if they are "bad," the rains stop. One can hardly miss the sexual overtones that more than allude to the role of the male in impregnating the female. Moreover, the sex metaphor is reminiscent of the various fertility cults of the people during the days of the First Commonwealth. Yahweh, of course, abhors these cults.

In Genesis, as in the rest of the Bible, the references to the land are numerous and are also correlated with sex, fertility, and morality. The connection between land (earth) and proper moral behavior can be seen in God's bringing about total destruction in the flood because "the land was filled with iniquity" (6:13). In a story that has Hebraic consequences (Judah and Tamar), Er spills his seed "to the land" (38:9) in a conscious effort to deny Tamar an heir; Yahweh is displeased with Er's act and kills him. Whether the displeasure is related to a Hebrew law that is being violated by Er or whether Yahweh's rage is indeed a statement against goddess worship,[17] the link with the land is firmly effected.

Land finally becomes territory for which men go to war not only because it is the source of life and livelihood but because it is a symbol of power, possessions, and pride. From a male's point of view, there is very little difference between land and women. Both function for very similar purposes; both slowly evolve as objects of contention for which men, if necessary, will fight. The first man in Genesis was given dominion over the land (1:26) as well as over the woman (3:16b). War, which was not part of that initial control, enters the picture with the "cutting" of the covenant with the first Hebrew patriarch (chap. 15), who is told by Yahweh that Canaan will eventually be his. Punishment and terror against the inhabitants of the land accompany the covenantal promise. In the story of Dinah, revenge is exacted when a virgin is violated, not because of the emotional (or physical) scars inflicted on the woman but because a whole family's future and possessions seem to be under attack.

The background of Dinah's story is made up of the story of the return of the house of Jacob to Canaan. The significance of the move from Laban's home back to Jacob's place of birth is underscored by the main protagonist's transformational experience, in which he acquires a new name (Israel) and a new personality (ironically, he limps away from his encounter with God), both of which enable him to face his once-hostile brother. As soon as Jacob/Israel settled his accounts with Esau, he continued on his way to the vicinity of Shechem, where he bought a parcel of land from Hamor (33:19). He also built an altar which he named "El, the God of Israel" (33:20). Settlement of Canaan is thus firmly linked with the God of Israel, who under the guise of Yahweh cut a covenant with Abraham, Jacob's grandfather. The land motif coupled with the promise to the fathers of the tribe is indeed an appropriate introduction to the story of Dinah.

Finally, the story of Dinah begins before the first verse of chap. 34. She was born to the matriarch Leah at the end of her second cycle of births (30:21), and she was treated very casually when she came into that world. Unlike the six sons that precede her, Dinah's birth is recorded as: "and she [Leah] bore a daughter, and she named her Dinah." All of the fanfare and emotion that Leah invested in the birth of her sons was missing when Dinah arrived. More important, immediately after the birth of Dinah, the text narrates in a rather climactic fashion the birth of Joseph, Rachel's first son. Not only is Rachel finally relieved from her "shame" (30:23), but Jacob decides that it is now time to leave his father-in-law's house and return to Canaan. Dinah's structural position in the household is indicative of her social stature at the moment of birth and later on: she is surrounded by the birth of Leah's sixth son, whom Leah rejoices in tremendously, thanking God for his birth (v. 20), and the birth of Rachel's first son, with whom she is so overjoyed that she too, like her sister before, turns to God for thanks (two references to God are made in the text: one to Elohim, who "removes" Rachel's shame, and the other to Yahweh, who hopefully will "add" another son [vv. 23-24]). Dinah's birth has not been asked or called for; she has no specific place within the house even though she is Leah's last born and, from a matrilineal point of view, extremely important. Leah's expression of particular joy at the birth of Zebulun may be an indication of her special feelings for a son whom she might have considered the last born. When Jacob finally makes his move, it is related to the birth of Joseph and is narrated as a climactic ending to a journey that started with the strife with Esau (the older son who was rejected by Rebekah and Isaac). Dinah is not the one who determines continuity in the house of Jacob; instead, Joseph, who is ultimately the beloved son, becomes a powerful political figure who saves his family—including presumably Dinah, who is taken with the family to Egypt at the end of Genesis—at the right time. Expressed differently, Dinah's appearance on the family's horizons is marked by way of a footnote; Zebulun's birth—and even more so Joseph's—is an event of almost cosmic proportions that causes great change in the affairs of the whole household. Indeed, when Dinah is born she remains almost hidden within the tent, but when Joseph enters, Jacob starts moving toward higher and better things. Dinah's lot, as well as the lot of the other Genesis matriarchs, is ultimately the tent; Joseph's and the other men's fortunes are outside of it.

The Plan of the Study

The book is divided into five chapters: Chapter 1 sets up the framework for the tale of Dinah with a general discussion of the position of women in Genesis. It stresses the women's dependence on the men, highlighting the issue of childbearing and focusing on the apparent paradox that one of the most overwhelming occurrences in the text is the inability of the major women-matriarchs to have children. Childbearing—or the inability to bear children—illuminates the puzzle of women's powerlessness in Genesis as well as informs about the social and familial priorities of the text. Both society and family left their indelible mark on Jewish history.

Chapter 2 is a comparative study of Eve and Dinah, underscoring the redactors' perspective, which called for the description of women as sexually oriented. In this analysis, Eve will be viewed as the representative of all womankind, while Dinah will be seen as a symbolic warning to other Israelite women not to socialize with non-Israelites. Both Eve and Dinah are handled by the narrators as transgressors who made an effort to widen the realm of their experiences and in the process offended patriarchal values. They were brutally and swiftly placed where they belonged. Eve's story finally echoed the story of the Hebrew people, who abandoned the commands of their God and lost their Eden/Canaan. Dinah's tale evolved into a nationalistic parable of exclusion with the Hivites functioning as the Canaanite "strangers" and enemies whom the redactors abhorred.

Chapter 3 juxtaposes two important matriarchs, Rebekah and Rachel, with Dinah. It highlights the distinctive images used in Genesis to differentiate between the men and the women. In line with that gender separation, it will be demonstrated that the authors create a landscape whereby the world outside is described as full of treachery for women who therefore need to be protected by the males. In this controlled environment, the women are viewed as basically weak and dependent. To assist them to overcome their intrinsic weaknesses, the males lay out an elaborate protective shield, insisting that women who are ready to accept their protection will be safe and content. Rebekah and Rachel seem to play by the patriarchs' rules and therefore appear to function successfully, albeit marginally, from within the tent. Dinah's narrative, which is dark and violent, serves as a stark example of the foreboding outside. Her rape is portrayed both as the result of her unthoughtful behavior and as an instant punishment for disobeying the rules spelled out by the men of the tribe.

Chapter 4 consists of an analysis of the story of Dinah. The most important aspects of the narrative will be accounted for: for example, the physical violence (rape) that was inflicted on Dinah and its implications; the psychological damage that she suffered as a result of the rape and its aftermath; as well as the social ruin, which was the most cruel of all and which doomed her to a life of eternal isolation. The motif of circumcision will be properly assessed in relation to the brothers' wish to avenge Dinah's rape, as well as in connection with her ultimate well-being. Finally, Dinah will be recognized as a woman who tried to socialize in a new environment, but because she encountered a non-Hebrew who finally wished to marry her, her destiny assumed moral and political dimensions. Accordingly, Dinah's misfortune was transformed into a warning to women about the dangers, personal and familial, that lurk outside of the house.

Chapter 5 is an attempt to analyze the Dinah affair from a contemporary, political perspective. Issues of exclusivity as well as separation will be emphasized and placed within a larger cultural framework. For example, it will be shown that the idea of the covenant introduced into the Hebraic equation fierce elements that sometimes contradicted more noble beliefs. In addition, we will see that although the concept of the covenant laid out the ground for a superb philosophy of dialogue and understanding, it also furnished and encouraged questionable positions about morality and political behavior which had a lasting impact on Jews and Western civilization alike.

In a concluding section, the dark aspects of monotheistic faith will be reevaluated in an attempt to place the concept of a "chosen" people in a more exclusive perspective. It will be argued that a corruption in nationalistic aspirations leads to a diminishing of fortunes for "strangers" as well as for women. Finally, it will be maintained that in order to alleviate somewhat the lot of the powerless and the excluded, it is essential to look at Dinah in a new light. She must be studied now as an active political figure who tried to steer the Hebrews away from brutal confrontations. Her "going out" must be understood as wise and desirable. Even though the redacted Dinah was silenced, it is now possible to endow her contemporary counterpart with a voice that would enable her to complete what the original Dinah wished to attain. Since she was heading in the direction of socialization and cooperation, since she was curious about "the daughters of the land," she was willing, in Buber's terms, to "become a self with the other."[18] Indeed, Dinah could serve as a model for many Israeli women who struggle to form a coherent political, pacifistic group with an agenda of Palestinian accommodation.

The heart of this book is the story of Dinah in Genesis 34 and what it tells us about the various characters within the text and the various authors of the text. In the appendix, I attempt to reconstruct "The 'Other' Text," that is to say, the story of Dinah not as we have it, but in its unredacted, reconstructed state, which is indeed a very different story after all.

Throughout this study, the translations are my own and the references are directly to the Masoretic Text (Bible in Hebrew), which occasionally differs by a verse or two from the numbering of verses in the standard English translations of the Bible.

NOTES

1. The word *mōhar* occurs only three times in the Bible: Gen 34:12, the story under consideration; Exod 22:16, which is expressed legally and in binding terms; 1 Sam 18:25, which is the story of Saul's attempt, by his demand for the foreskins of Philistines, to topple David, the poor shepherd, who cannot afford the *mōhar* for the princess, Michal. See Roland de Vaux's treatment of the institution of *mōhar* in *Ancient Israel: Social Institutions* (New York: McGraw-Hill, 1965) 1: 26-27.

2. See E. A. Speiser, *Genesis* (Anchor Bible 1; Garden City, NY: Doubleday, 1964) 267.

3. Traditionally, the most overtly monarchic story was that of Judah and Tamar, at the end of which the twins that are borne by the woman are directly associated with the house of David (chap. 38). But more recently J. A. Soggin has discussed political elements in Genesis, for example, the promise of a kingdom to Abraham (12:2) and to Judah (49:10), which he parallels with Nathan's promises to David (2 Sam 7:9 and 7:12ff.) (*Introduction to the Old Testament,* trans. J. Bowden [Philadelphia: Westminster, 1976]). Likewise, R. E. Clements argues that the covenant with Abraham was developed as a model for David's attempt to unify the Israelites (*Abraham and David* [Philadelphia: Fortress, 1963]). See also David Damrosch, *The Narrative Covenant* (San Francisco: Harper and Row, 1987), particularly chap. 4: "Yahwist(s) and Deuteronomist(s)," which outlines the development of Hebrew Historiography and the early monarchy.

4. According to E. A. Speiser's commentary on this chapter, "Shechem was inhabited at the time by Hurrian elements" rather than Hivites (*Genesis,* ad loc.). Speiser suggests that not only does the text support that claim (e.g., that the "Hivites" are presumably uncircumcised, in contrast to other Canaanite tribes, but "cuneiform records from the region of Central Palestine have shown that Hurrians were prominent there during the Amarna age (ca. 1400 B.C.)." It is thus quite possible that the narrative in this chapter (34) details a rift that must have occurred between the Jacobites and the Horites (as the Septuagint refers to them). In that context, the presumed "history" of the affair dates back to pre-exodus times "and very likely prior to Amarna times" (p. 267).

5. See the arguments of the various commentators in Frank McConnell (ed.), *The Bible and the Narrative Tradition* (New York: Oxford University Press, 1986). McConnell, in his introduction (pp. 3-18) suggests that the main tension of biblical narratives is indeed between the gnosis and nostos.

6. R. de Vaux, *Ancient Israel,* 1: 186-87.

7. Moses' mother and sister (Miriam?), as well as the various midwives and the daughter of the pharaoh, are quite extraordinary, active women, who contribute decisively to the success of the exodus.

8. Martin Buber, *Israel and the World* (New York: Schocken Books, 1965) 222.

9. Ibid., 225.

10. Martin Buber, *Between Man and Man* (trans. R. G. Smith; New York: Macmillan, 1965) 170.

11. Buber, *Israel and the World*, 193.

12. Rabbi Meir Kahane, *Our Challenge: The Chosen Land* (Radnor, PA: Chilton, 1974) 42.

13. The redactors' concern for survival, which first of all stems from their own experiences, is also a reflection of the classical prophets' concerns during the eighth century B.C.E. There is no question but that the prophetic movement as a whole can be seen as a response to looming catastrophes and as an attempt to achieve communal survival. If one were to focus on this particular motif (survival) in the prophets' ideology, one might conclude that indeed they were the first redactors who wished to place the Israelite experience within a larger perspective. They therefore made a conscious effort to commit their prophecies to writing, as if declaring that "to replace land and government, temple and palace, the cities and villages and farms which made up Israel and Judah, there had to be a Bible: a book which would embody all those things, relate history and justify the ways of God to people. . . . This is what made the prophets of the eighth century 'writing' prophets: the imminence of the crisis and its aftermath" (F. I. Andersen and D. N. Freedman, "Introduction" in *Hosea* [Anchor Bible 24; Garden City, NY: Doubleday, 1980] 42). In view of the Assyrian destruction of 722 and in conjunction with the more total Babylonian devastation, the sixth-century redactors attempted to internalize both disasters and emerged with a synthesis that they hoped would prevent assimilation (which happened to the northern tribes) and assure continuity.

14. Even the fact that the Hebrew noun for "land" is female in gender is quite significant.

15. It is significant that even in an eschatologically oriented chapter, where the prophet praised the new harmonious and close relationship between Yahweh and the people, the terminology of people, land, and women's sterility was still used. Thus, Isaiah's poetic outburst which glorifies the people's restoration to their land was articulated as: "Sing, barren one, who has not borne; break out merrily in song you who has not been in labor" (54:1). Echoing the barrenness motif in Genesis, the prophet uses the metaphor in a much more overtly patriarchal manner especially when he emphasizes the dismal past, "the shame of your youth . . . the dishonor of your widowhood . . ." (v. 4).

16. Rosemary Radford Ruether (ed.), *Religion and Sexism* (New York: Simon & Schuster, 1974).

17. Tamar, in this very esoteric story, seems to operate as a priestess who serves as a fertility goddess surrogate. Er's spilling his seed is actually a statement about his ability to commune with the priestess. The son's death is brought about by Judah, the patriarch who is concerned about the rights of his sons over against the power of his daughter-in-law. When she finally lures him, she is also in the guise of a priestess-whore (*qĕdēšâ-zōnâ*).

18. Maurice Friedman, "Dialogue, Confirmation, and the Image of the Human," *Journal of Humanistic Psychology* 28 (1988) 125.

1

THE POSITION OF
WOMEN IN GENESIS

Patriarchal Ideal versus Matriarchal Reality

READERS OF GENESIS have been struck by a major issue that keeps recurring in the various narrated sagas, namely, that even though the text is of a patriarchal orientation, all of its significant women seem to be quite powerful, even if that power is of a "domestic" sort. Moreover, although center stage is reserved for the patriarchs and their male descendants, paradoxically the matriarchs and their favored children almost always prevail. For example, although the text promotes a patrilineal succession, whereby the firstborn has full rights and privileges, the narratives are pervaded by a matrilineal reality. The child favored by the mother, regardless of birth order, finally becomes the major inheritor not only of possessions and material goods but of the covenantal promise, which is at the heart of the Hebraic heritage.

The male protagonists who fill the pages of the book are mainly the Hebrew patriarchs, who originated in Mesopotamia and migrated to Canaan at the command of Yahweh. The main concern of the patriarchs is twofold: how to become established in the new land and how to continue the family line. Because of this dual interest, the overriding issue of the book is legitimacy, namely, who is the legitimate heir and how does one provide for that heir? A side issue, clearly linked with the question of legitimacy is the establishment of residency in Canaan, the land Yahweh promised to Abraham. The writers as well as the final editors and redactors of Genesis did not shy away from admitting that the Hebrews had no tangible claim to Canaan and, in key stories and episodes, they subtly, but firmly, search for an authentic validation of that claim.[1] A combination of circumstances, environment, and spiritual inclinations led all of those involved in constructing the book of Genesis (and particularly the redactors) to Yahweh, the God that they fully embraced and that they claimed "gave" Canaan, as a covenantal endowment, to the Hebrews. We are thus told that since one cannot seriously question Yahweh's motives and because his is the whole world, he decided at a specific point in time to bestow a country on his beloved servant, Abraham. The book successfully establishes a familial and a social order, ideally connected to God. At the point of their convergence, the familial and the social form the background for a complex ideology that is land-oriented, hierarchical, and patriarchal.

How did women fit into that larger framework? There is no easy answer to this question because, as in the case of other complex issues raised in the text, one must account for the various revisions, representing historical layers, that Genesis has undergone. Added to that is the ultimate issue of redaction, which must be taken into consideration for a better insight into the stories. Although it is not our explicit task to summarize current trends in biblical scholarship, nor is it our intention to break new ground, and/or find new solutions, in the area of final compilation, redaction, and canonization of the text[2] it is our assignment to examine more carefully the mind of the editors and redactors of the book in order better to understand the position that women had to accept within Genesis as well as, ultimately, within Jewish society.

Part of this examination will lead us into the realm of "strangers" and their role in Genesis and other parts of the Hebrew Scriptures. Ultimately, this study will show that there is a clear link between women and strangers and that they were assigned to marginal positions within the Hebraic social order because they were perceived as ideologically weak and untrustworthy.

Narrative Sources

Kingly Sympathizers

The notion that there were at least two major narrative sources that left their mark on the various stories of Genesis is plausible and defensible. The first narrative source is associated with a group of scribes and/or priests who were affiliated with the court and the kingship, particularly the house of David/Solomon, during the period of the First Hebrew Commonwealth (tenth to sixth century B.C.E.). The second source probably originated with a group of ideological leaders who appeared on the Judaic scene after the destruction of the Commonwealth and during the time of the Babylonian Exile (sixth to fourth century B.C.E.). The writers associated with this source were loyal to a monotheistic God whose precepts, they declared, were handed down to the Jews by the prophet/lawgiver, Moses; sometimes the latter group is referred to as Deuteronomists.[3]

The first group of compilers was affiliated with the court of the presumed popular kings, David and Solomon, and because of these ties, their stories were slanted in the court's direction, underscoring an authoritarian, legalistic, orderly, and ritualistic point of view: authoritarian, highlighting the absolute power of the king; legalistic, stressing the entrenchment of that power and the desire to perpetuate it for as long as possible; orderly, accentuating the strong belief that order in the universe means goodness;[4] ritualistic, detailing the symbols, insignia, pomp, and circumstance, dear to kings and their subjects, all of which serve as symbols of closeness between tyrants and their followers. Examples that reflect the general orientation of this authorial group follow.

Stories of absolute power abound in Genesis: from God's pronouncement that the man will "rule" over the woman (3:16b), using terms that are taken directly from the political realm, to a more economically focused tale where Joseph is afforded almost boundless power in order to assure the survival of Egypt (41:40–44).

Stories that are legalistically inclined consist of incidents of land purchase completed by public fiat, which was equal to signing and verifying official documents (23:16–19), as well as stories about the legal status of adopted children and/or the obligations of a brother vis-à-vis a widowed sister-in-law.[5]

A strong sense of order is projected in the text when it details the story of the creation of the cosmos in seven days (chap. 1). Each day is meticulously accounted for, and the progression of the narrative, from the most abstract (the creation of light) to the most concrete (the creation of people) lends the unit an aura of simple but orderly credibility. It further advances the narrators' position as rational and essentially anthropocentric.

Even in a very important narrative (chap. 38), which could easily have been appropriated into the realm of didactic, personal, and familial moralizing, the authors transform the focal point of the tale (Judah's sleeping with his daughter-in-law) into an incident about a desperate woman who tries to retain a sense of order and stability. The morality of Judah's affair with Tamar, with whom he actually commits incest, is not the main issue of the chapter. Instead, when the moment of truth arrives and Judah is forced to recognize that Tamar was trying to perform a familial duty and that he had forsaken his obligations as father-in-law, he merely admits that "she was more right than I" (v. 26).[6] This underemphasizes the sheer immorality of his behavior but reiterates the book's commitment to an orderly society. It is worthwhile to recall that King David, whom the text perceives to be a descendant of the tribe of Judah, could have been indirectly implicated in this questionable affair. But the encounter between Judah and Tamar develops as a genealogical tale complete with the birth of twins, the younger of whom (Perez) forces his way out in order to be recognized as the firstborn. Indeed, one cannot miss the link with the house of David nor, indeed, the implication that Judah's abandonment of order — that is, his neglect of his daughter-in-law and its concomitant ramifications — is the most vital consideration in the text. Tamar's actions (reminiscent of Ruth[7]) are upheld as worthy and correct because she was the agent of order in the story as well as the mother who finally gave birth to an important pair of twins. Stated differently, even in a story that could have become morally "messy," the redactors stay the course typical of the whole of the text. Although it is not the task of this study to explore the personality of Tamar, it must be noted that, given her Canaanite roots and her possible links with fertility cults (see how Judah refers to her both as $z\bar{o}n\hat{a}$ [whore] and $q\check{e}d\bar{e}\check{s}\hat{a}$ [holy prostitute], 38:15, 21), she is one of the most independent and courageous women in the Hebraic tradition. It is possible that precisely because she was not a Hebrew, she was allowed to act the way she did.

There are many ritualistic tales dealing with matters fundamental to the well-being of any society. The courtship ritual is highlighted and the ritual of hosting and protecting guests' security.

Both of these ritualized behaviors reinforce the vulnerability of women: in the courting ritual the men pull the strings almost every step of the way, and in their zealous attempts to assure the security of "wayfarers for the night," women sometimes lose their own security (19:7–8).[8]

In the larger perspective of courtly sympathizers, rituals that celebrated an orderly rule helped to entrench further those who were portrayed as, and perceived to be, the protectors of the people. In this particular context, the actions of Simeon and Levi in the story of Dinah are simply another example of the maintenance of family order and stability. In fact, the rape of a woman (particularly a virgin) in an androcentric society had economic and psychological ramifications that demanded a precise response, because the males of the family had all of their future invested in a woman's virginity. Even more directly, the story of the rape of Dinah is reminiscent of the story of the rape of Tamar, King David's daughter, who was avenged by her brother Absalom. The overwhelming importance of the court's sympathizers was in their ability to link certain political realities with mythology. There is no question but that David and Solomon destroyed the traditional tribal structure, associated with the early Hebrew settlement of Canaan (see particularly Joshua and the judges). Yet, as David Biale had already observed, the new theory created by the court's theologians "portrayed David and his dynasty as the adopted sons of God, thus adding a familial touch to the traditional language of election."[9] Biale goes on to conclude that this link between the kingship of David and the mythology of the elected community further legitimized the king's rule and provided it with a strong, secure base.

Deuteronomists

The second group of narrators who were heavily involved with the redaction and compilation of Genesis, the Deuteronomists, was even more ideologically oriented than the first. To understand their position, it is important to acknowledge the debt that they owe to the classical prophets (eighth to sixth century B.C.E.). But since the Deuteronomists operated in a completely different environment from that of the Davidic scribes or the classical prophets, their concerns were dissimilar as well. Their postexilic vantage point (sixth century B.C.E. and beyond) demanded that they redact stories that could also be used as ideological weapons. In particular, the Deuteronomists were looking for means by which they could establish the best social, political, and psychological landscape for a community in dispersion. In other words, it was important for the Babylonian Deuteronomistic redactors to place the disaster of exile, which they experienced firsthand, within a reasonable context; in fact, they finally elevated the state of exile into a moral value, claiming that it was the ultimate graphic manifestation of a historical process that began when Yahweh revealed himself to the greatest of all prophets, Moses. That revelation led to a redemptive act (exodus from Egypt) that culminated in the people's settlement in the "land of milk and honey." But, the Deuteronomists argued, the Israelites of the First Commonwealth degenerated into a people who gave in to their evil impulses (with the help of women who led them astray), abandoned their God, started to worship other gods (and goddesses) and were punished by Yahweh for their indiscretions. In the first powerful myth in Genesis, the first woman was associated with symbols of the goddess (serpent, trees, and rivers). By rejecting the act of eating the forbidden fruit — or by presenting it as a disobedience to Yahweh — the narrators rejected the goddess. By claiming that it was bad, particularly by hinting that it diverted attention from the Tree of Life and its promises of immortality, they linked women with evil and a base sort of mortality.

Similarly, the prophets, who were radical monotheists, would not accept any other god or goddess; they preached exclusivity on all levels and claimed that they continued in the footsteps of Moses, who first introduced Yahweh to the Israelite tradition.[10] The fact that Yahweh was associated with typical male values, like land acquisition, was no accident, and the further advancement of Yahweh meant, at the very least, harping on themes like women's inferiority.

The prophets also liked to focus on the institution of marriage as a symbol of fidelity and commitment. From their perspective, the woman was unfaithful and the man constant in his commitment. For example, Hosea's initial calling was associated with a marriage to a whore, which he converted into a major symbol of the relationship between Yahweh and his people — Yahweh being the loyal husband/lover and the people fulfilling the role of the whoring wife.[11] In the Jeremiah tradition, we find a similar analogy: ". . . you, who have whored with hosts of lovers. . . . Where have you not been lain with? By the roads you sat waiting for them like an Arab in the desert. You have polluted the land with your whorish depravity" (3:1b–2). In line with the objectification of women in the text, it is significant that the punishment pronounced on the "whore" is this: "So the showers were withheld, and the spring rains never came. But yours was the harlot's shameless brow, you refused to be abashed" (v. 3). And even more poignantly, ". . . she polluted the land, committing adultery with stones and trees" (v. 9b). When the prophet reproaches the people collectively, he finally settles on referring to them as "the daughter of Zion"; the woman and the environment become one, thus completing the objectifying process.[12] There is no doubt about the impact of the prophets on the Deuteronomistic redactors of the text and, in turn, the latter's concept of the role of women in the universe and, more directly, in Israelite society.

As for the exilic, environmental impact, the redactors were products of an era that linked successes or the lack thereof with a supernatural entity. They were also in the midst of a political landscape which, while tolerating a variety of peoples and religions, did not encourage nationalism and uniqueness. Moreover, because of their Jewish, "defeated" status, they had to fit into a more general framework of other "conquered" peoples, which blurred the distinction between them, their God, and others and their gods. An environment of this kind was much more conducive to assimilation and nondistinctness. Hence, from the early days of the diaspora, it was important for all those related to the leadership of the Jewish community, and particularly the Deuteronomists, to establish unique power characteristics that would be automatically associated with monotheism. To that end, it was essential to create a tapestry of symbols and rituals that would emphasize the special aspects of Yahweh and his cult. In other words, once the Deuteronomists embraced Yahweh as their one and only God, there was a clear move on their part to institutionalize an ideology and to focus on a variety of concrete symbols that helped the Judeans in Babylonia to rally around them politically. For example, houses of worship (synagogues) were established to substitute for the ruined Jerusalem temple. There was a demand to be present regularly in those shrines so that Yahweh could be worshiped by the whole community. A "pure" posture and rituals of purification (actual as well as symbolic) were of the utmost significance.[13] More and more, the political prestige of the Deuteronomists was linked to an emphasis on Jewish exclusivity as articulated by the God of the covenant. Jewish purity of heart was contrasted with shady motives manifested by the other nations, who did not recognize the supremacy of Yahweh.

But for a variety of reasons, an emphasis on cleansing and purification was almost always accompanied by a negative attitude toward women, who were perceived, universally and particularly, to be essentially "unclean."[14] Uncleanness and the idea that abandoning Yahweh and worshiping "the Queen of Heaven" (Jer 44:3–22) was one of the major reasons for the destruction of Israel in the first place did not bode well for women — especially since women were perceived as the major contributors to goddess cults. The Deuteronomistic genius was thus similar to that of the Davidic scribes and theologians; it offered a synthesis of mythology and reality which was so compelling that it was fully accepted by the tradition as solid history which, in turn, became the so-called Jewish posture.[15]

The Conniving Matriarchs

At best the status of women in Genesis is ambiguous, and at worst their position is totally dependent on men. Indeed, it is very difficult to find even one coherent story that tells of a woman who was completely independent, self-confident, or self assured. Again and again, the narrators point out that women, when they were active, were operating as the shadows of men, whether fathers, husbands, or brothers.

The most important "business" of women in Genesis is childbearing and therefore their most devastating situation was childlessness. Barrenness, in addition to pointing to a woman's essential weakness and vulnerability, evolved as a larger symbol of women's inferiority. When Sarah cannot bear children, she resorts to a practice that finally dehumanizes her and her maid. In fact, Sarah's mistreatment of Hagar (Gen 16:6) is so severe that the slave not only earns the sympathy of the reader but, what is more significant, receives a direct message from the angel of God, who tells her to return to her mistress and continue to be abused. Sarah's relative power over Hagar deteriorates into an ugly conflict over basic rights and securities and does not enhance either woman's image. But the angel who interferes seems to punctuate the ugliness rather than solve the problems of Hagar. The confrontation between Sarah and her handmaid is intriguing in so many ways that it has led to a host of scholarly points of view, some condemning Sarah's behavior and others supporting her.[16] In a larger historical framework, the animosity between the two women typically developed as the acute enmity between their sons, Ishmael and Isaac. The narrators took a very clear position, which excluded Ishmael and his mother and offered Isaac the covenantal inheritance; they also depicted Hagar as an Egyptian in an attempt to place her within a mythically charged predicament. In many ways, the episode describing the complex relationship between Sarah and Hagar is an ironic reversal of the greater episode recounted in the book of Exodus, where the Israelites are the slaves and the Egyptians, the abusing masters. The Sarah–Hagar feud is subsumed into the conflict between their sons, and the women are pushed to the background while the men take over.

In another incident, Rebekah uses trickery to assure the inheritance to her beloved son (Gen 25:26–27; 27) and in the process denies Esau what presumably belongs to him. Like Ishmael before, Esau is ultimately portrayed as the loser (who later on in the tradition is recognized as a "stranger") in a fight which involves the future of a nation, its supreme deity, and the land promised by him. It is no accident that the rancor involving the issues of legitimacy and inheritance is closely tied to women. The narrators, with significant help from the redactors, thus succeeded in emphasizing the disruptive elements that they perceived to have been at the heart of all womanly activities. Even the most sympathetic of women in Genesis, Rachel, has to endure the fate of a barren wife, constantly competing for the attention of her husband. And although there is no doubt that Rachel is the beloved wife and that her sons (when they finally arrive in the world) have a bright future in store, there is a tragic ending to the Rachel portion of the story. In a way, Rachel's death, while giving birth to her second son, Benjamin (35:17–18), bolsters the argument that the most notable role for women is biological and that they live and die only as biologically determined people.

The Move to Canaan

Since childbearing is the main womanly agenda of Genesis, it draws our attention to the social and familial priorities of the text. The Hebraic family delineated in the book is an extended household attempting to foster firm links with a new land. The process of staking residency claims in Canaan led the family of Abraham to examine more thoroughly those who were already inhabiting the country. The interactions with the local residents were not extensive, as reported in the text, but they did occur. There were some bonds that were not looked upon favorably and that were tied to family continuity and stability which the Hebrews limited to their original habitat, presumably in Mesopotamia. The restriction, first articulated by Abraham (chap. 23), meant that Isaac (and later on, Jacob) had to look for a wife outside of Canaan. It also meant that the woman who was finally selected had to be uprooted from a Mesopotamian environment, which was not like the Canaanite realm.[17] A change in environment, always a difficult proposition for anyone, man or woman, meant a modification in life-style and an adjustment to a different mode of existence. The text delineates the change as fundamentally new to the men, but it does not dwell on the meaning of the transition to Canaan for women; nor does it comment on their reaction to the transfer. Accordingly, the "call" to Abram is not matched with a call to his wife, Sarai, even though she ultimately joins him.

There is very little information about the position that Hebrew women might have enjoyed in their original homeland and whether or not the move to Canaan might have affected them negatively—or maybe even turn out to be the source of their undoing.[18] A survey of the various patriarchal sagas from the woman's point of view hints at the possibility that indeed women had undergone a change in life-style as well as in status. The text features at least two distinct episodes which confirm the notion that women had had in the past some authority—more significant than what is narrated in Genesis. The first example is that of Sarah and her maidservant, Hagar. For better or worse, Sarah is presented in the text as having total independence with regard to Hagar; in fact, she could even determine whether the servant remained in the house or not. Moreover, Abraham, who strenuously objected to his wife's treatment of

Hagar and his firstborn son, does not prevail in this episode. It is not clear where Sarah's power came from: was it merely her individual strength, or was it a remnant of an era when women had more power culturally and even legally? The text is silent about everything associated with the life of the Hebrews before they came to Canaan, even though it clearly demonstrates that their sojourn in Canaan is not the starting point of their history and that they did carry with them values that were from another culture and another time.[19]

The second example of women's independence, or at least more positive status, is in the encounter between Eliezer and the males of the house of Laban when he asks for Rebekah's hand for Isaac. One of their responses is that she has to decide whether she wants to join him or not. The text narrates two responses, one of which is typically authoritative: "Here is Rebekah before you, take [her] and go" (24:51b); the other response is more tolerant of the woman as a person: "Let us call the maiden and ask her" (24:57b). This example is not an extreme one, but it does point to a measure of willful independence that women enjoyed before they actually departed for Canaan (Rebekah is about to leave her mother's and brothers' house in this episode).[20]

The environmental change, from Mesopotamia to Canaan, was a radical turning point in the life and history of Hebrew men, who were subsequently granted the Yahwistic covenant; but for the women of Genesis—if indeed the Rebekah sequence is indicative of anything—the move signified an erosion in status. The patriarchs were heading toward wider horizons and entrenchment in a new land; the matriarchs were steered in a more narrow, inward direction. The narrators go to great lengths to describe, literally and figuratively, the meaning of the change that the families from Ur and Haran undergo. Although the women join the men and are shown as supporting the journey's effort, the males are the heroic voyagers: they confront the great issues of displacement and reinstatement. Even when they do consult with their women, it is for purposes of corroboration rather than concrete counsel.

Yahweh, who commands Abram to move to Canaan, is portrayed in the text as a powerful God whose ultimate act of grace is to "cut" covenants with his followers as a way of maintaining a close relationship with them. In some cases he does side with the women, but by and large he tends to communicate only with the males.

Sisters and Maid-servants

The text also deals with women other than mothers or wives. There are sisters (Rachel and Leah as well as Dinah) who seem to function in a very nebulous world of brothers and fathers who are aggressive, vengeful, and fiercely competitive. Once again, because of the essentially male orientation of the text, there is very little information about the bonds between sisters or, for that matter, bonds between brothers and sisters. Genesis makes reference to some sister–brother relationships that evolve into central episodes with overwhelming ramifications.[21] At the same time, though, those relationships are not very well developed, and the little information we do have leads in the direction of tension and violence. Although the "brother" seems to take charge of the fate of his sister (as in both the Laban and Simeon and Levi stories) at a crucial point in her life (just before she is ready to start a life of her own with another man), he is also portrayed as concerned about the economic fate of the family. Laban is throughout the text the devious manipulator always ready to make a profit; Simeon and Levi end up with material profits as well.

The dubious position of maidservants within Hebraic society is also portrayed in Genesis. What rights, if any, did maidservants have? Does the text tell us stories about women slaves in order to reinforce the main notions associated with the other, more important, women (or men) in the text? Or does the text focus on the maidservants for other purposes? Could a person (male or female) perpetrate more violence on a maidservant just because of her social and economic dependence? We can draw some conclusions about the privileges and obligations of maids in the text, but there is still much that needs to be explored. There is no doubt, though, that in the case of at least three of the matriarchs—Sarah, Leah, and Rachel—maidservants played a pivotal role in the home and ultimately contributed to the physical, if not spiritual, makeup of the Hebrew people.[22]

* * *

The overall impression created in the text is that women were the weak link in a chain that had to rely on men for daily survival. Women are portrayed as vulnerable on two counts: first, their mental makeup: they tend to be swayed very easily and do not recognize danger right away. Second, they are physically weak and need the protection of strong males. Women were credited with waywardness and transgression not only in the religious sense but in the familial as well. For example, the woman in the Garden of Eden roamed around and found the serpent, who led her and everyone else to disaster. Physical weakness is the hallmark of Dinah's affair; she is "taken" by Shechem who then proceeds to rape her. There are also more subtle weaknesses of women pointed out by the narrators, as will be shown further on.

Before drawing any conclusions about women's weaknesses, it is important to note that women's flaws are underscored by violent acts portrayed in the text. Genesis emphasizes violence in a politically ideological context and, in the final analysis, links it with the role that "strangers" and the inhabitants of Canaan fulfill. Violence against women (and Canaanites) was presented by the narrators as an element of communal cohesion and redemption; as such it was condoned. It should be further noted that the term "violence" includes the mental, verbal, and psychological abuse more than outright physical injury, although the latter is clearly displayed in the book as well, especially when discussing the "inhabitants."

In an ideologically charged environment, when the survival of the whole nation was presumably at stake, there was a tendency to focus on selected groups of people who were designated as carriers of special burdens. Women, because of their childbearing capacity, almost always became "special" in that sense. But if the ideology demanded that the survival of the people be linked to territorial conquests, women were then called upon to assure the survival of the nation in the most intimately physical way. Not only were they then referred to as the nurturers of society; they also turned into "breeders," who had to be protected from real and imagined dangers. When that need arose, it was a double-edged sword: on the one hand, pronouncing the quasi-magical qualities of women was also recognizing their mysterious power; on the other hand, the same qualities may lead to an underscoring of the males' desire heavily to "protect" women's magic. This, in turn, may lead to a denial of liberties and an essential perception of women's weakness and fragility. The rise of patriarchy did not erase the former attitude but it did contribute to the latter. The rise of national ideologies polarized the community along gender lines: women became "weaker vessels" that had to be assigned safe havens and that had to be guarded by strong men whose role was to protect them from all enemies, real and imagined. In that sense, there is an unmistakable affinity between women and "strangers" in the nationalistic élan, to the detriment of both.

NOTES

1. Even though Genesis does not deal with the conquest of Canaan, the narrators are very much aware of the ethical issues involved in a conquest of this kind. In a major pre-Abrahamic tale, the narrative focuses on Noah and his family after the flood; in that tale (which is still subject to furious scholarly debate) Canaan, the son of Ham, is cursed by Noah because his father committed an unspeakably immoral act (Gen 9:22–27).

2. For a better understanding of the problems involved in these issues, the reader may wish to turn to E. A. Speiser's introduction in *Genesis* (Anchor Bible 1; Garden City, NY: Doubleday, 1964).

3. For a detailed discussion of this group, specifically its indebtedness to the prophetic tradition, see R. P. Carroll, *From Chaos to Covenant* (New York: Crossroad, 1981). For a literary historical analysis of the Deuteronomists and their impact on the whole of the Hexateuch, see R. Polzin, *Moses and the Deuteronomist* (New York: Seabury, 1980).

4. It is interesting to read Phyllis Trible's analysis of the story of the concubine of Ramah (Judges 19) from that particular perspective; she makes the point that disorder and acts of terror (which seemed to have been rampant during the days of the Judges) were juxtaposed, by the voice of the text, with law and order (*Texts of Terror* [Philadelphia: Fortress, 1984]). From a woman's perspective, the irony is that when order is brought about by the kings (who follow the judges), the attitude toward women does not change very markedly.

5. Compare the motif of child adoption as practiced by Sarah and the other matriarchs with some of the legal provisions for adoption in the laws of Hammurabi; see S. J. Teubal, *Sarah the Priestess* (Athens, OH: Swallow Press, 1984). As for the institution of Yibum (levirate marriage), i.e., marrying one's brother's widow to produce offspring, the Pentateuch and the book of Ruth are quite clear on the subject.

6. It must be remembered that chap. 38 tells a self-contained story about Judah and his household; in so doing, the narrative flow of the story of Joseph, which starts in chap. 37, is interrupted. Classical commentators already drew attention to that narrative break and suggested that the

reasons for it had to do with the power of Judah, who emerged as the leader among the brothers. Further, the story of Judah, which is also the story of Tamar, his daughter-in-law turned whore turned Judah's consort, ends on a note of family continuity that is directly related to King David. See also Ruth 4. The role of the Canaanite environment in both stories is stressed, which has led some to conclude that there must have been a significant amount of Israelite assimilation into Canaan before (maybe even during) David's reign. Other scholars go so far as to maintain that the Hebrews left no significant original mark before the eighth century B.C.E. (the rise of the classical prophets); see specifically Giovanni Garbini, *History and Ideology in Ancient Israel* (trans. John Bowden; Suffolk: SCM, 1988) 1–32.

7. See the remarks of Edward F. Campbell, Jr., about covenant and law in the book of Ruth; he argues that the text projects a communal interest above a purely personal one, which places the main characters within a more compelling framework of communal order that is important to uphold (*Ruth* [Anchor Bible 7; Garden City, NY: Doubleday, 1975] 30–33).

8. On a more subtle level, when the case for a strong authoritarian center is made in the book of Judges, there is a confrontation between the concept of order (and, by implication, morality) and that of disorder (and immorality). Judges uses the expression "doing what is right in your eyes" to mean an immoral anarchy that leads to general debasement and the collapse of all values (the story of the concubine of Ramah is particularly acute). Presumably, the establishment of judges and later on kings led to a healing which was beneficial to all members of society.

9. David Biale, *Power and Powerlessness in Jewish History* (New York: Schocken Books, 1987) 30.

10. See specifically the still very convincing arguments made by Yehezkel Kaufmann in his classic *History of the Religion of Israel from Antiquity to the End of the Second Temple* (in Hebrew) (Tel Aviv, 1956).

11. For an analysis of the connection between the contribution of the prophets and the Deuteronomists, see Joseph Blenkinsopp, *Prophecy and Canon* (Notre Dame, IN: University of Notre Dame Press, 1977); of particular interest are chaps. 4 ("No Prophet Like Moses"), 5 ("The Making of the Prophetic Canon"), and 6 ("The Transformation of Prophecy").

12. See also T. Drorah Setel, "Prophets and Pornography: Female Sexual Imagery in Hosea," in *Feminist Interpretation of the Bible,* ed. Letty M. Russell (Philadelphia: Westminster, 1985) 86–95.

13. The combination of houses of worship and purification rites helped promote the segregation of women, who were systematically pushed to the background of synagogue rituals until finally a "veil" went up to exclude them almost totally.

14. Ezekiel was the major exilic prophet and, more than any other prophet, emphasized the ritualistically unclean condition of women. Ezekiel was particularly concerned with blood imagery in its relation to

women and their "natural" polluted existence; see especially chaps. 13 and 16.

15. One should always bear in mind the fact that the Babylonian-Deuteronomist point of view represents only a small segment of what finally emerged as "Judaism"; in that sense, the Babylonian triumph is only part of a much larger process, which finally materialized as the Jewish tradition. See Carroll's comments in chap. 9, "After the Fall: Exiles and 'Exiles,'" *From Chaos to Covenant*, 226–48.

16. For the former, see Trible, *Texts of Terror;* for the latter, L. Ginzberg, *The Legends of the Jews* (Philadelphia: Jewish Publication Society, 1968) 1:263–64. The folk tradition goes so far as to maintain that Sarah's positive influence was so significant that her ". . . death was a loss not only for Abraham and his family, but for the whole country. So long as she was alive, all went well in the land. After her death confusion ensued" (p. 287). The approaches that favor Sarah emphasize the legitimacy of her son and treat Ishmael as a second-class person, in line with Deuteronomistic ideology, which emphasizes the cause of the Hebrews as related to Isaac.

17. See Teubal, *Sarah the Priestess,* 19–41, where the difference between Canaanite and Mesopotamian traditions is stressed and evaluated.

18. Ibid.

19. The best introduction to the patriarchs' background is still W. F. Albright, *Yahweh and the Gods of Canaan* (Garden City, NY: Doubleday, 1968); see specifically, section II "The Patriarchal Background of Israel's Faith," 53–109.

20. See Teubal, *Sarah the Priestess.*

21. For example, Rebekah and Laban, who also seem to share some negative, manipulative traits; and Dinah and her brothers, who, even though there are no other references to interactions between them, must have had something in common.

22. Reference must be made to the major tribes that the tradition claims owed their origins to Zilpah and Bilhah. Also, the very fact that Reuben decided to "violate" the privacy of his father's bed by sleeping with Bilhah suggests that she had clout in the house because of her ability to bear children, as well as because of her links with Rachel. She may also have had some power of her own that we are not aware of.

2

EVE AND DINAH:
THE ROAD FROM
EXCLUSION TO EXCLUSIVITY

Violence in Paradise

THE FIRST NARRATED act of violence perpetrated on a woman in Genesis is recorded in the first story about people in the book. The first woman (later on referred to as Eve) was "cursed" by the male God of the Garden of Eden, who was outraged by her explicit disobedience of his command not to eat of the fruit of the tree of knowledge. There are two distinct realms of punishment that Yahweh identifies while proceeding with the curse: the first is purely biological and places the woman within a physical context (bearing children in pain) that is debilitating, if not life-threatening; the second is related to the woman's position *vis-à-vis* her man (Adam), according to which, the "curse" maintains, she will "desire him" and thus become fully dependent on him. Although the text uses language that is clearly sexual (*wě'el 'îšēk těšûqātēk*, "your desire is to your man" [Gen 3:16]), it implies that "desire" in the context of that punishment is social (v. 16b) as well as economic. This is further reinforced when compared with the punishment/curse pronounced on the man, who shared the fruit with the woman and who was doomed to work the land by "the sweat of his brow." The man is "condemned" to go out of the home and be more closely associated with work, which is not domestic, even though it is hard. He is also instructed to cultivate a special relationship with the soil, which ultimately produces pain for him. In other words, the man is heading outside of the garden and into an open world, whereas the woman is heading in the direction of closure. Significantly, there is no suggestion that he become dependent on her (unlike the other narrated version of the relationship between man and woman [2:24], where it is suggested that a man shall "cleave" to his wife and thus become "one flesh"). On the contrary, it seems that leaving the woman behind to go to work the soil is an attempt on the part of the man to become free of womanly associations and perhaps find another way of relating to and harmonizing with the earth from which both of them originated. Stated differently, even though there is pronounced violence in the curse placed on the man, it is coupled with an attempt to divorce him from what might have been a closer, and a more equal, association with the woman. Indeed, even though he is now dependent on the soil for his survival, he is also the new master ($m\bar{o}\check{s}\bar{e}l$) of the woman. This version of the story is of utmost significance because, as was just mentioned, it sharply contrasts with a similar passage in chap. 2, where the man and the woman are perceived as one unit and where the editorial commentary suggests that "this is why a man shall leave his father and his mother and will cleave to his wife, and they will be (become) one flesh" (2:24).[1]

Eve and the Redactors

The story of the garden sets the tone for the rest of Genesis. The people who emerge out of Eden (typically a term that connotes pleasure in the sexual sense) are portrayed as basically weak and dependent, either on each other, as in the case of the woman, or on other forces. They are instructed to involve themselves in a struggle that underscores their political and social status. In a sense, they define their realms of experience and dominance first of all as physically related and, second, as socially viable. The woman emerges totally dependent on her biological capabilities, and her main function is to bear children—in pain, no less. Further, she, more than he, seems to depend on her sexual identity; in fact, she is the one who desires sexual contact and he is to "rule" over her. Sex is used here in the context of manipulative power, where the woman is inferior to the man in the most fundamental human realm. Although both of them are commanded to "propagate and fill the earth," the curse that is placed on the woman diverts attention to the absolute function of the male: he is the one who determines propagation and the woman is his tool. There is deep anger expressed by the God of the story, who is disappointed in his creatures but also determined that they will not reach the state of immortality. For that purpose he places the "revolving fiery sword" in front of the tree of life to make sure that the humans are denied an essential segment of the divine.[2] Violent images are thus piled up as an expression of revenge and vindictiveness, though they all finally point to the "transgression" of the woman, whose discourse with the serpent evolved into a most fateful act.

The story of the garden brought into focus the basic sexuality of the woman in a framework that denigrated and enslaved her. Sexual desire became the woman's vocation because without it she could not fulfill her destiny, which was also the destiny of the whole species. Sexual desire became her trap because while engaging in sexual intercourse, which is perceived by the text to be only procreational, she pointed to her social position, namely, her subjugation to the man.

Why is it that even though both people committed the same crime, one of them (the woman) was singled out for a punishment that called for her withdrawal into the house and exclusion from public life, while the other (the man) was sent into the world? Also, since the story indeed is about sexuality (they both found out that they were "naked" after they ate of the fruit of the tree of knowledge) and sexual awareness,[3] why does Eve have to be identified by sex more than her mate? The narrative points to Eve's presumed capitulation to the "cunning" serpent, but it is important to place the episode within a cultural and political framework—which harks back to the task that was undertaken by the redactors of the original oral myth.[4]

The Redactors and the Garden of Eden

From the postexilic, redactive vantage point (sixth-century B.C.E. and beyond), the story of the garden was of fundamental importance because it provided a weapon that was used by those ideologues who were looking for means by which they could establish the best social, political, psychological, and ideological landscape for a community in dispersion. In other words, it was important for the redactors to place the disaster of exile within a reasonable, Hebraic context. Eve was thus presented as the first woman who was created by the God that the Babylonian redactors fully embraced. She was also described as the first person to disobey that God and at the most promising point in history, namely, when everything seemed to have been in a state of perfection and harmony. As others have already pointed out, it is no accident that the story of the garden incorporates water and river imagery. Indeed, the myth is closely associated with Babylonian sources, and the whole sequence of birth, closeness with God, disobedience, and punishment is suspiciously reminiscent of the great mythology which unfolded around the history of the Israelites, who saw themselves as having been taken out of their Egyptian exile and brought (by Yahweh) into the land of milk and honey (a paradisal environment), Canaan (Israel). They then worshiped God for a brief period of time, but after a while they abandoned him and were ultimately punished for this abandonment.[5] By no coincidence, we are told in Genesis that an exile of Abraham's descendants will occur and that Yahweh will redeem the "seed of Abram" (15:13) so as to bring the terms of the covenant to full fruition.

Because of the redactors' frame of mind and environmental circumstances, they highlighted the Hebrews' enslavement to the Egyptians; it supplied them with a great mythology which contained political elements and accentuated the greatness of Yahweh, who transformed the Hebrews from slaves to free people. As a nation that owed allegiance to Yahweh, the Hebrews, according to the redacted text, were adamant about their political agenda. Moses' messianic mission was quickly seized by Joshua, the judges, and the kings. The destruction wrought by the Babylonians enabled the redactors to reiterate the terms of the Mosaic revolution so as to emphasize the stipulations of a covenant that was not simply a dialogue between the deity and the people but a nationalistic contract replete with territorial rights and war campaigns.

Thus it was that the significance of the whole history and mythology of the children of Israel was encapsulated in the story of the Garden of Eden, as the Babylonian redactors perceived it. In a masterly stroke they edited a seminal myth, the surface of which told about humankind's transition from innocence to experience, so as to fit it perfectly into their own universe of loss and sorrow. They projected their own environment onto the story of the garden, within which they made room for Yahweh and his two creatures/ people who began their relationship in harmony and agreement but ended in disarray. Moreover, the close bond between the people and their maker collapsed because of the woman, who was curious, naïve, stupid, gullible, naturally unreliable, or even plainly bad. Similarly, the Israelites of the First Hebrew Commonwealth, who finally gave in to their evil impulses (presumably with the help of women who led them astray), abandoned their God, started to worship other gods (and goddesses), and were punished for their indiscretions.

Eve's role as a model for the later Hebrews is at once subtle and propagandistic: the subtlety is in her very position in the garden — she is a "helpmate" to the man. Actually, she is brought into being from his body,[6] a detail that sharply contrasts with the various rituals and ideas of the fertility cults and the role of woman in "giving life" to all. But she finds herself entangled with the serpent, who is traditionally associated with images of foreign gods and fertility rites.

Within an Israelite perspective, there is a connection between Eve and the prophetic approach whereby the Hebrews were presumably the "brides" and close associates of Yahweh but found themselves (especially in Canaan) involved with other deities. Even though Eve is not portrayed as an Israelite or a Hebrew (she simply is "every-woman"), in the story of the garden the redactors set up a universal framework which was the first step to claiming that all women, regardless of national origin, were particularly vulnerable on issues of loyalty and fidelity.[7] The road from this point to a more specific one about Israelite women and infidelity is fairly clear, particularly with the "threatening" advent in Babylonia of assimilation by mixed marriages. Even though it can be argued that the Hebraic experience, before the appearance of redactors and textual editors, evolved from a variety of confrontations that could have been perceived as assimilationist in nature, it is only after the destruction of the First Temple and the phenomenon of the first exile that assimilation became a central issue in Jewish ideology. Ezra is very careful to argue the case against "the peoples of the lands" and their "contamination" of the "holy race" (chap. 9), and even though his appeal to the community does not center only on the wrongdoings of Hebrew women, it rests on the assumption that "uncleanness" in its sexual, familial manifestations must be uprooted. Ezra's argument, which prefaced a "purging" of foreign women, ultimately became a rallying cry for those who pledged themselves to a particularistic agenda based on "clean" blood and the belief in Yawheh as the one and only God. Ironically and not by accident, the Hebrew patriarchs in Genesis were also concerned about tribal continuity and attempted to retain closeness and tradition by providing their sons with marriageable daughters from their own tribe and family.

Canaan: The New Garden of Eden

When the Hebrew family of Abram is introduced in Genesis, the theme of Yahweh's commitment, established by the narrators of the Adam and Eve story, is further expanded in the account of the first major patriarch, Abraham, who is instructed by Yahweh to move from Mesopotamia to Canaan. The move marks the beginning of a new life for Abraham, and in the context of a new life, Canaan constitutes a new Eden.

The theme of Canaan as the new Eden—that is, the promised land—continues with the generation of Isaac, who takes Rebekah as his wife. We may recall that, like Sarah, Rebekah too was uprooted from her home in Haran and brought, by Abraham's loyal manager/ servant, to Canaan to start a family of her own. In fact, Isaac's acceptance of Rebekah into the "tent" of his mother Sarah was accomplished as one of the last significant acts of Abraham, who sent his trusted slave to look for a bride for his son. The text thus implies that the tradition started by Abraham was continued, under his careful supervision, by Isaac. Abraham's authority in the text is significant, and the narrators wish to make it absolutely certain that Isaac stays within the confines of that authority and continues in his father's footsteps.

The exile that occurred in the Garden of Eden and that led to a distancing of people from God is only dimly remembered in the

Abrahamic sagas. The Hebrews are portrayed as the new people chosen by Yahweh for a specific purpose, and just as Yahweh had instructed the first man and woman with certain tasks and duties, he directs Abraham to fulfill a few obligations. The premise that was established in Eden stayed intact in all of the patriarchal chronicles, and the new "chosen"[8] were to enjoy a blissful relationship with a God who guaranteed them land and prosperity. The pledge was embodied in a covenant sealed (signed) in the cutting of the male's foreskin, and the promised land was Canaan.

Circumcision — Preliminaries

Circumcision is a major symbol of the change in the environment of the Hebrew males and their relationship with God, but it also must be examined within the context of the violence inflicted on women (and later on the "uncircumcised"). First, Yahweh's demand that the males in a household be circumcised alienated the men from the women. In other words, circumcision, which was the sign of the covenantal link between men and God, was also the sign that separated them from women, and the separation of the sexes is a familiar motif in Genesis. Estrangement occurred in the garden, where the man and the woman were treated differently after they transgressed the divine command not to eat of the fruit of the tree, and this different treatment focused on their sexual function. Likewise, when Yahweh offered the covenant to Abraham, he chose a "sign" that, in addition to being associated with initiation rites, was also — maybe, mainly — connected to sexuality. Ironically, the "sign" is related to a most painful (one can say that it is inflicted cruelly), violent act, which is used by Jews to this very day, to signal belonging and "tribal" affiliation. The woman's exclusion from participating in a ritual that focuses attention on God's beloved children may have begun with circumcision, but it is a problem that increased in severity throughout Jewish history.[9]

In the story of Dinah, circumcision (or the nonobservance of it) plays a pivotal role not only in relation to the woman but also in reference to the stranger. The narrators draw attention to the "strangeness" of the Hivites by pointing to their lack of circumcision. But contrary to the other circumcision episodes, in the Dinah narrative this ritual functions as a punishment inflicted on the Hivites by the brothers of the violated woman. The penalty, though, quickly results in a violation. Indeed, the brothers punish the perpetrator(s) of the crime against their sister, but they also violate their own integrity when they claim that vengeance is their only motive. In fact, their plan to attack their sister's rapist, especially when viewed in the context of the social mores of the ancient world, is an attack on the ultimate well-being of Dinah, who as a nonvirgin will find it very hard to establish a family of her own. Moreover, she is never consulted by them (compare the consultation that, in at least one narrative version, transpired before Rebekah was dispatched to become the wife of Isaac), nor does she play a part in any of the events that take place after her initial departure from the house. On one level the brothers seem to admonish Dinah for leaving the house without asking for permission, but on another level — perhaps a deeper one — they are making sure that she does not gain anything, material or spiritual, from her attempt "to go out." Punishing the rapist may have been the right moral thing to do, but forcing the woman back into the house leads one to reflect on the issue of women's security and happiness. In other words, if Dinah is brought back to the brothers' tent in order to spend the rest of her life there in isolation and shame, was she really well served? The question is even more acute within a strictly patriarchal structure where so much rides on the woman's virginity. We have seen in the story of the woman in the garden that a similar question arose, namely, was Eve a beneficiary of the banishment from the garden, especially when banishment was accompanied by condemnation to a life of dependence on her man?

Male Violence in the Eve and Dinah Narratives

Did Eve and Dinah achieve ultimate security as a result of the actions of various males taken in their behalf? It is obvious that the men were well served. In the case of the garden, the man was pronounced the master over the woman's fate, thus acquiring a measure of power. In the Dinah matter, the brothers gained possessions and land that they did not have before their sister's "outing." Violence was used in the case of the woman banished from Eden, and terror

was undertaken in the case of Dinah. In both cases, the violence was
not directly aimed at the women. On the contrary, other parties
suffered physically much more: the serpent in the garden underwent
a physical transformation for the worse, and the Hivites in Canaan
were literally slaughtered. Yet Eve and Dinah are etched in memory
as the main participants of both affairs.

The posture of alienation between the serpent and the woman
came about as a result of God's dissatisfaction with the actions of
the woman. Enmity between the Hebrews and the Canaanites was
an ideological requirement that was accompanied by a rational conviction on the part of the redactors that the Canaanites' involvement
with "other" gods and goddesses was immoral. Although the story
of Dinah is not about "foreign" worship, it is about a cruel form of
exclusion: the woman is excluded from participating in social functions outside of the home without the permission of the men
because people outside of the home are described as dangerous and
prone to vicious attacks. The woman is believed to be too weak —
perhaps too unreliable — to handle peril. In the tale of Dinah, the
redactors stop short of openly advocating that those who are not
Israelite, not circumcised, and worship other gods are dangerous to
the community and have to be eradicated. They leave the literary
framework which describes the acts of Simeon and Levi in as dreadful a format as possible, and they also maintain the literary ambi-
guity which is posited at the end of the tale and which leaves much
of the moral judgment to the audience's interpretation.[10]

From the perspective of postexilic Judaism, which fretted much
more about the fate of the community than the individual, Dinah
was dangerous because she asserted herself as a woman with a
distinct identity. When she "goes out" of her father's house, she is
alone and unaccompanied by any of the traditional signals other
women use when they undertake similar "departures." Those missing
signals, in the context of the period of the return to Zion (534 B.C.E.
on), turned Dinah's story into a parable with a deep moral lesson for
the whole Jewish population, but particularly for women. The redactors deliberately retained the narrative's connection with the story of
the rape of Tamar (2 Samuel 13),[11] which suggests that there was an
old tradition — perhaps an oral source — that contained a rape story
associated with a sister who was abused and then avenged by a

compassionate brother (see the role of Absalom in the Tamar trauma [2 Sam 13:22, 28, 32]). The similarities between these two stories are many, but the differences are even more striking. For example, in the Dinah story the prince who rapes the woman is not a half brother but a Hivite outsider/stranger. In the story of Tamar, Absalom, who is the sly perpetrator of violence on Amnon, ultimately limits his revenge to Amnon alone, thus engaging in exact retribution, unlike the brothers in Genesis. Furthermore, Absalom flees from David's palace, afraid that the king's wrath will bring havoc upon his (Absalom's) life. Nothing of this kind happens to Simeon and Levi, even though Jacob does register his displeasure with their acts. These and other differences bring out the public aspect of the story of Dinah, a feature that points to the redactors' agenda and their concern with educating the public about women and violence and strangers.

Dinah was presented in Genesis as a woman who tried to socialize in a new environment; but because she encountered a non-Hebrew — even though he finally wished to marry her — her fortunes diminished. The narrators treat Dinah as a fragile being, reminding their audience that women are vulnerable. The narrators are particularly careful to point to Dinah's age at the time of the rape: she is a *yaldâ*, "a child," as well as a *na'ărâ*, "a girl." The issue of her youth alludes to her basic innocence and inexperience, echoing the situation of the woman in the garden, and places a premium on her "marketability" as a potential virgin-wife. After the rape, not only does her personal condition change, but her social status is radically altered (as we are explicitly told in the other rape story, 2 Sam 13:20b).

Dinah's youth and implied weakness called for her brothers' intervention, but the fact that the person forcing the issue of her frailty was a stranger complicated matters. Shechem's "strangeness," in the redactive milieu, was a political battle cry, and the brothers don the garments of exclusion and communal blood purity. The whole affair was thus transformed into the realm of power politics, portraying Jewish individuals when confronted with national adversity. Accordingly, Dinah's misfortune was reconstructed into a warning to women about the dangers that lurk outside of the house, and the brothers' operation further reinforced the Deuteronomistic notion that if it takes violence to secure a country, so be it.[12]

Eve and Dinah: Rebels and Transgressors

Eve and Dinah function in their respective stories as the representatives of an ideologically oriented group of people who had a clear communal, nationalistic message. Eve is portrayed as the representative of all womankind; Dinah is a symbol and a warning to other Israelite women. From the redactors' point of view, both of them have transgressed quite severely: the first disobeyed God and subsequently led all of humankind out of the garden; the other left her father's house and as a result was raped by a Canaanite foreigner. The first woman was "deceived" by the serpent, but only because she was away from the protective surroundings of her male. Dinah was violated by a Canaanite rapist who took advantage of her vulnerability, namely, her age and her being outside of the father's and brothers' shelter. The implication in the text is that both of these women had a home where they belonged; both had certain provisions that dictated to them how to behave and what to do. For example, the woman in the garden (along with her man) was supposed to "guard" the garden; Dinah was supposed to stay in the house until, by males' standards, it was safe to emerge. Both of them rebelled; the first woman, in a very direct manner, openly departed from the command of God; Dinah went out of the house without first consulting with the males.

What unites the two women is their departure from the norms that were set up by the men: in Eden the woman challenges God's command to refrain from eating the fruit and, more important, the command not to "know," whether sexually or rationally. In many ways, the woman's rebellion is a declaration against ignorance and manipulation by the powers that be, as well as an assertion against excluding those who hold different opinions. The woman in the garden is ready to converse with the serpent, who convinces her that "the fruit is good to eat" (3:6). When she experiences that "goodness," she immediately shares it with her man. It is the ominous appearance of Yahweh Elohim which interjects discord, suspicion, shame, and exclusion. Dinah goes out to associate with the Hivites; like the woman in Eden, she is playing the game of inclusion, while the brothers' response is exclusion.

Eve's story sets the stage for Dinah's tale because it insinuates that women are unreliable and therefore have to be kept under strict scrutiny. The latter story is more directly related to a uniquely Jewish situation, which addresses the issue of mixed marriages and, even more blatantly, the ideological question of exclusivity in its relation to Yahweh and the covenant that he "cut" with the community of Israelites. But just like Eve, who lost her independence and freedom of mobility when she dared go against Yahweh's command, Dinah too lost her mobility as well as her future, because she sought company outside of her father's house and among those that Yahweh forbade the Hebrews to associate with. Dinah's relationship with the Hivites was taboo for postexilic Jews, and they painstakingly claimed that Israelites should marry their own kind and stay within the limits of the divine covenant, which excluded all those who were "uncircumcised."[13]

* * *

The redactive agenda, which undoubtedly was survival oriented, included a strong nationalistic prescription that called for land, law, and a central government. The land was Canaan/Israel/Judea, and the law was Mosaic, as grasped by the Deuteronomists. Intrinsic to the law was a stipulation that identified Hebraic/Jewish government as kingly and priestly. It was the king's obligation to pledge security to the people as well as to provide them with reasonable borders within which they could live happily ever after. It was the duty of the priest to preside over the ritual that reminded people of Yahweh and his absolute function within Jewish society. The Mosaic law instilled pride within the males of the community for accepting a spot in the cosmos which was created and governed by the mighty Yahweh. In fact, everyone who accepted the lordship of Yahweh finally found a definite role to fill, including women. But the function of women turned out to be extremely limited and very heavily dependent on the males. It was the strong sense of destiny, signified in the covenant, coupled with nationalistic pride (belonging to the "chosen" community) that spelled suppression for Hebrew women. Although women were recognized as having the power to breed and perpetuate the race, they were also perceived as being in need of protection. Their sexuality, as the narrators articulated it, played an essential role in their lives: from Eve, who dared to eat of the fruit that made her "knowledgeable" about her body, to Dinah who "went out," explicitly or implicitly, in order to be seduced. Because of Eve, claimed the redactors, people lost their Eden. Because of Dinah, in the redactors' mind, the Hebrews could have potentially lost their uniqueness. Eve was finally controlled by the curse of God, who placed her under the watchful eye of her man. Dinah was snatched out of the house of her tormentor and returned to the house where the brothers were carefully watching.

The violence of the curse of Yahweh in the garden narrative should not be underestimated; neither should the violence inflicted on Dinah. Eve's story paved the way for limitations that were placed on the simplest of women's actions, namely, whom to have sex with and when.[14] Dinah's tale paved the way for severe restrictions on the freedom of Hebrew women to decide for themselves about their futures and to move out of the house. In the long run, the success of both these stories and their implied messages lies in the role of the "stranger," who was identified with a sinister corrupting force particularly appealing to women. The woman in the garden was lured by the serpent, who delivered a message antithetical to that of Yahweh. Dinah attempted to merge her fate with the Hivites, contrary to Yahweh's covenantal demands. Both women were brought down to earth, isolation, and silence.

NOTES

1. The best attempt at a positive interpretation of this particular passage is still Phyllis Trible's, "Depatriarchalizing in Biblical Interpretation," in *The Jewish Woman: New Perspectives,* ed. E. Koltun (New York: Schocken Books, 1976).

2. Zohar Kabbalists have already made the point that the most significant aspect of the transgression in Eden was the violation of the basic balance of the universe. The woman's indiscretion (or sin) was her focusing only on the tree of knowledge and overlooking the tree of life. For the Kabbalists it was inherently important to stress that both trees were in "the midst of the garden," which suggests that there was a certain unity in the initial creation that should not have been violated.

3. On the issue of sexual awareness and the eating of the fruit of the tree of knowledge (as well as the general sexual context of the episode) there

are numerous commentaries: in the Midrash, for example, the tree is said to have had the power to increase desire. Later commentators dwelled on the connection between the serpent and Eve to her detriment; e.g., Wolfgang Lederer sees the serpent as a sexual symbol, and thus the affinity between the woman and the serpent as basically sexual and negative (*The Fear of Woman* [New York: Harcourt, 1968] 47–49). See also Katharine M. Rogers, *The Troublesome Helpmate: A History of Misogyny in Literature* (Seattle: University of Washington Press, 1973) 3–23. For a more positive approach to the tree, Eve, and sexuality, see Trible, "Depatriarchalizing. . . ."

4. See J. A. Phillips, *Eve: The History of an Idea* (San Francisco: Harper & Row, 1984): "The Mother Goddess of ancient Near Eastern religions, by whatever name she was called, was honored and worshiped with the title 'the Mother of All the Living.' According to Genesis, this is the meaning of Hawwah, or Eve, the name given by Adam to the first woman" (p. 3). Phillips goes on to say that in the process of demythologizing the goddess, the writers of the text presented Eve as the first woman. And because all parties fulfill their roles adequately, the story's ending is positive. Whether the redactors of the text may have aspired to that type of demythology or not is at best debatable, but it is clear that they succeeded in focusing on the woman's role in the eating of the fruit as pivotal to the whole process of life and survival.

5. Both G. E. Mendenhall (*The Tenth Generation* [Baltimore: Johns Hopkins University Press, 1973]) and David Noel Freedman (*Pottery, Poetry, and Prophecy: Studies in Early Hebrew Poetry* [Winona Lake, IN: Eisenbrauns, 1980] 167–78) question the authenticity and accuracy of the "history" recorded in Genesis and elsewhere in the Pentateuch. R. P. Carroll attempts to link the concept of Israelite fate and "history" with a clear theodicy which maintains that the God of Israel is a God who needs to be followed very strictly (*From Chaos to Covenant* [New York: Crossroad, 1981]); otherwise he will take revenge. But before that revenge is executed, God will send his prophets to warn the people about their transgressions and the possibility of repentance.

6. One should still pay attention to the imagistic impact of this particular scene in the garden, where the woman is portrayed as the most intimate partner of the man. This must be further underscored because of the normally frivolous attempts to view the woman as "clearly" subordinate to the man because of the fact that she "was taken from his rib."

7. In order to see how the classical prophets present their arguments regarding women, one should examine especially Hosea and Jeremiah. There is a personal tone of anxiety which projects the prophets' personal trauma into the public arena; thus, Hosea, who, so he claims, had been rejected by his wife, portrays her as a whore, who, he claims, is similar to all Israelite women. They supposedly sleep with other men and worship

other *bēʿālîm*. In other words, Hosea deliberately confuses a ritualistic commitment to the cult of Baal and Astarte (Asherah) with a personal betrayal.

8. The concept of "chosen," even if not mentioned as such, is an important one in Hebrew Scriptures. After the first couple loses Eden and after people "corrupt" the earth, God centers his attention on Noah, who is "chosen" to inherit the earth.

9. Examples of erosion in women's status and participation in Jewish communal life abound in Jewish history. The classic reference is in the Prayer Book, where the man is instructed to say every day: "I thank You, O Lord, that Thou hath not made me a woman."

10. It is significant that the Dinah narrative ends with a question: "Will our sister be treated like a whore?"

11. In the case of Tamar, who was raped by the prince Amnon, the heir to David's throne, there was a passion that preceded the main event and was described by the narrators as "great love." (P. Trible has argued that "love" in this context should be translated "lust" (*Texts of Terror* [Philadelphia: Fortress, 1984]). After the rape, Amnon is described as "hating Tamar more than he loved her before" (v. 15). This is, of course, diametrically opposed to the Dinah story, where Shechem is said to have fallen in love with the girl only after he raped her. See also Yair Zakovitch, "Assimilation in Biblical Narratives," in *Empirical Models for Biblical Criticism*, ed. J. H. Tigay (Philadelphia: University of Pennsylvania Press, 1985) 189.

12. Even though the tone of the narrative generally disapproves of the deeds of the brothers, the attitudes of commentators throughout the ages have varied. Some have been positive about the brothers' revenge, blaming Dinah for any hint of immorality. In intertestamental literature, there is only one reference to the story; it is found in the book of Judith, at the time the heroine prays to God asking for help in the mission to dispose of Holofernes: "O Lord, the God of my ancestor Simeon, remember how you armed Simeon with a sword to take revenge on those foreigners who seized Dinah, who was a virgin, tore off her clothes, and defiled her" (9:2-4). Judith's version, which is understandably propagandistic, adds so many awful details to the encounter between the Hivites and Dinah that the brothers who undertook the plundering and the murders emerge as saviors operating under God's commands. *Midrash Rabbah* (London: Soncino, 1983) claims that "Simeon and Levi acted in Shechem with a reason. . . . And what caused this? The fact that the daughter of Leah went out" (2:736).

13. The concept of "uncircumcised" eventually became a pejorative term, and it is already used as such by Jeremiah (4:4, referring to the community's "uncircumcised heart," and 6:10, in the phrase "uncircumcised ear"). Dinah's story legitimizes the use of force for purposes of keeping people out of the vicinity of the "holy" community. It also implies that there

is something fundamentally flawed and immoral in those who are uncircumcised. Finally, for a Jew, the uncircumcised become affiliated with the uncivilized, dark forces of the universe. See how Bernard Malamud used the phrase "uncircumcised dog" in *The Assistant* (New York: Avon, 1963); ironically, Frank Alpine (the major protagonist of the novel) falls in love with Helen (Morris Bober's daughter), whom he ultimately rapes. Helen's reaction to Frank's deed is summed up by her outcry: "uncircumcised dog."

14. The post-Eden text clearly says that she will desire her man and he will rule her, which implies that these decisions are in his hand.

3

INSIDE OR OUTSIDE THE TENT: WHITHER WOMEN'S SECURITY?

Gender Relations in Genesis

DINAH'S TALE must now be examined within a more limited setting; particularly, it is important to probe the narrative's relationship or the lack of it to other stories involving Hebrew women in Genesis. In that context, Dinah must be compared with those women who were more successful than she was in acquiring a man. Because the process of becoming established for purposes of procreation and tribal continuity is at the heart of Genesis, it is important first to study the text's general approach to male–female relationships.

The overall redactive, patriarchal design was to divest women of whatever power they had and to relegate them to a very specific corner—"the tent" and its immediate correlation with procreation. Indeed, the narrators of the text focused on a variety of stories that dealt with male–female relationships. They told tales about the two genders' free interactions; there was neither forced marriage (except in one of the most ironic plots, where the male, Jacob, was deceived and led to a "bed" he did not want to sleep in) nor union that was distasteful to any party. Further, the "romances" described in the text are quite tactfully handled, and at no time is the woman unaware of the identity of her future intended (which is not to say that all brides actually saw their grooms before they were married; e.g., Rebekah committed herself to an arduous journey and an unseen man).

The overall impression of these stories, in line with the rest of the text, is highly ideological and points to a rather detailed plan on the part of the redactors to set gender relationships within a context that will place the man in a clearly advantageous position vis-à-vis the woman. In this sense, the stories that follow the Eden account merely "fulfill" the curse that Yahweh placed on the relationship between men and women. Specifically, and in order further to emphasize the difference between the environments of men and women, the text depicts the world outside, which is the world of men, as hostile and dangerous for women and the world within, "the tent," as safe. The external world is portrayed as a world where "strangers" roam freely, where there is deception and violence that the women cannot handle but that the men can. Women are thus cast into a family framework which is perceived by the text to be protective but which limits the women to biological procreation.

The two major betrothal narratives, which describe two women (Rebekah and Rachel) leaving their homes and going outside, clearly suggest that the major reason for a woman to leave the security of the tent is a prospective suitor. Indeed, the betrothal narratives are highly ritualized and create an atmosphere of safety and stability for the women. These episodes also grant women a voice that sometimes expresses their willingness to join the men who pursue them.

The narratives depict the major beloved matriarchs as unable to bear children. The irony of matriarchal barrenness played into the hands of the writers, who described the infertile matriarchs as extremely vulnerable; because of barrenness, their position as women, certainly as matriarchs, was seriously undermined. The advantage to the males of the condition of female infertility becomes clear as the stories unfold and the males are described as generous people who tolerate and love their sterile women. The narrators also make it clear that it is the "fault" of the women for being barren. The men are depicted as seemingly able to have children with almost anyone except their "beloved" wives.[1]

The matriarchs' inability to become pregnant introduces a subtheme that further diminishes women's position in the text by harping on the fundamental deficiency of a woman without children. The subtheme pits one woman against another in a sexually competitive stance which leads to bitterness and jealousy. Rachel competes for Jacob's attention with her sister Leah, and Sarah banishes Hagar from the tent. Infertility is thus manipulated by the males, who further argue that the woman's world is the world of the tent. There she can vent her anger appropriately, even delegate sexual authority to other women and, if she is deserving, become pregnant too. Sarah's pregnancy at the age of ninety is the most intriguing episode in this genre, and it points to the "rightness" of the redactors' ideological effort, which placed Yahweh at the center of the Jewish agenda. From the redactors' point of view, the power of God was not limited to land and wars but encompassed fertility as well. In fact, Yahweh as a God who can assist a woman who cannot be helped by "natural" means (18:11–13) is crucial to the covenantal idea and is even more important to the establishment of a predominantly male power base.

Love is just as manipulative: the men "love" the women who cannot have children, and they do not love those who can reproduce. Thus, Leah is in the most ambiguous position: she bears Jacob numerous children, yet she is left with no power. In fact, she is the epitome of powerlessness in the text because she is neither loved nor heard. Stories affecting women in their relationships with men minimize women's importance by limiting their actions to a certain, confined environment, which in turn renders their actions trivial. Moreover, the narrators of the stories resort to ritualized language and performance, which place women within a framework that is governed by men. Hence, if any of the rituals are not performed to the man's satisfaction, the woman is to blame. Consequently, when a man goes out to court a woman, she has to comply with his rules from beginning to end or she will not get married. Thus, Rebekah and Rachel are portrayed as the heroic matriarchs, put on a pedestal for every woman to celebrate and imitate. But Dinah, who does not follow their lead and does not perform the ritual of engagement the way her predecessors did, has no voice at all.

Finally, we will see, by paying closer attention to the role of brothers and fathers in Genesis, that the text highlights some of the more problematic aspects of a society that pays heavy tribute to its patriarchs and their male successors. Not only is there a dehumanization process that takes its toll, but there is an excessive emphasis on structure and rituals that must be followed sometimes to the detriment of individual members. It should be noted that in the process of aspiring to create a distinctly Jewish community, the redactors of the text may have given up a portion of the individual's soul and compassion. Some of what the text unravels is poignant and frightening. It is poignant because the men and the women who toil in the stories are portrayed realistically, effectively accomplishing their goals. For example, Eliezer's twice-told story of his meeting with Rebekah could test an audience's patience, but he does come through as loyal and intense. It is frightening because there is a mechanical efficiency to the characters' exploits. For example, Jacob cunningly shapes his destiny and successfully maneuvers his way by hook and by crook. Even so, the men and the women in the narratives emerge as forceful figures who choose a certain life-style not only for reasons of expediency but as a function of ideology. Part of the ideological vision that slowly surfaces in the text is of a dangerous world outside and a safe home inside, with the men shielding the women against peril.[2]

In many ways, the family and the community, which were the hallmarks of many narratives in Genesis and became crucial to the development of a Jewish identity, were finally cast in a nonegalitarian mold. Because of the emphasis on male authoritarianism and because of the intense desire of Jews to remain unique and exclusive, communal concepts were finally transformed into nationalistic ideologies that proved to be the absolute downfall for women.[3] It should be stressed once again that, although the redactors put their stamp of approval on the strong national feelings that emerged out of Babylonia, they did not invent them. The narrators of the chronicles of David and Solomon waved the nationalistic flag in whose name the kings conquered great portions of land and even dedicated a temple to the God of the prophets. The strength of these kings, as articulated in their feats, was measured by their mythical popularity, which, as time went by, proved to have been significant. In fact, the kind of nationalism inspired by their recorded deeds was ultimately codified in a great messianic doctrine that became closely linked with the house of David. The prophets first enunciated the doctrine of a messiah who would be of the house of David and who would reign supreme over the nation (Isaiah 11). Throughout Jewish history and even within the State of Israel today there is still a strong link between national and messianic aspirations.

The analysis of this chapter will focus on three aspects found in the Genesis tales having to do with gender relations: (1) love and its role in the life of a Hebrew family, (2) the ritual of finding a wife and its impact on the behavior of women, and (3) the unbending fulfillment of the first and second aspects for purposes of controlling women's destiny. Rebekah and Rachel conduct their affairs within a society that seems to be in transition; they have to migrate from their homeland (Haran) to a new country (Canaan) in order to establish a family. Dinah too is in the midst of transition: her family (that is, Jacob and his wives and children) has just entered Canaan for purposes of settlement and has not yet found a niche for itself. Ironically, the Jacob/Israel clan at this point in the narrative is a "stranger" in the land of Canaan. By comparing and contrasting these three heroines and their circumstances, it will be possible to comprehend better the conditions that led to a diminishing of status for Hebrew women.

"Going Out"

There were three daughters/sisters in Genesis who "went out" or "came out" of their homes. Two of them, Rebekah and Rachel, headed in the direction of a well in order to draw water for themselves and/or for their flocks. Happily for these women, in addition to accomplishing all of the above, they also found their future husbands. Rebekah—in the most elaborate prototypical story in Genesis—seems to have been the most independent and the most admirable woman. She was not just "given" to Abraham's manager/slave/confidant; she was "consulted" by her brothers (and mother?), who, at least in one of the multiple versions of the story, were reluctant to give her away without her consent.[4] In addition to pointing to some of the accepted courting customs of the time, this particular gesture also shows Rebekah's strength and position in the household and, by implication, in society.

Rachel "came out" in a fashion similar to Rebekah and found Jacob, her future husband, by the well. He fell in love with her at first sight, and she brought him to the house of her father Laban just as Rebekah had in the other narrative. But whereas Eliezer got what he was looking for immediately, Jacob had to wait for fourteen years before Rachel was fully his wife—that is, without obligations to her father. Rachel, like Rebekah, acted as a shepherdess. Both of them were very beautiful and, of course, virgins. When Isaac finally encountered Rebekah, he brought her to the tent of Sarah, his mother, and loved her. Jacob, even though he fell in love with Rachel, was annoyed and aggravated by Laban and had to wait for Rachel for a long time. But, in the end, because his love was so great he prevailed (29:20) and the betrothal story ended happily.

In these two cases, the males control the courting ritual, which takes place in an environment that is seminomadic.[5] Men determined whether and whom the women would marry. Although the women sometimes had a voice in the matter, the final decision was the men's. The motivation for courtship was materialistic. Commentators have observed that Laban, for example, scrutinized the candidates for his daughter's hand carefully, trying to find someone with substantial wealth who would be able to contribute to the well-being of the whole family.[6] In that framework, the women had some slack, but the men set up the rules that had to be strictly observed.

Dinah "went out" of her father's house not to water the flock but to "see the daughters of the land" (34:1), which implied that she went out to socialize with people not of her own tribe. Dinah's act was thus somewhat different from those of the previous matriarchs; the outcome was also different. Nevertheless, since Dinah's story is a "going out" story, it ought to be viewed in that light, namely, courtship. Accordingly, she too could conceivably have gone out, like her former compatriots, in search of a future husband. In fact, in one of the most ironic twists in Genesis, this is indeed what happened to Dinah: she did find a prospective husband. But the manner in which she accomplished what Rebekah and Rachel had accomplished before her was very different; the whole "outing" resulted in disaster for Dinah and her family.

Love and Betrothal

The various accounts of men courting women in Genesis are not typical "love" stories, but they do contain an element of love that leads to marriage and the establishment of a family. In line with the cosmic order outlined at the time of creation, which called on people to "multiply and inhabit the earth" (1:28), and in accordance with Yahweh's promise to Abraham (15:5), children play an enormous role in the narratives of Genesis. Thus, forming a family is an obligation associated with Yahweh, who himself becomes "engaged" and even "marries" his chosen bride, the people of Israel.[7] In many ways the family that is installed by God on earth reflects a divine order. When the classical prophets of the eighth–sixth centuries B.C.E. insist on the Israelites' fidelity to the covenant, they are portraying Yahweh as the loyal lover and husband and are pressing for monogamous relationships. But there is no monogamy in Genesis. Nevertheless, the fact that even the early patriarchs, who had more than one wife, preferred one woman is in line with the later prophetic and redactive ideology of monogamy.

As a sign of their love and commitment, women transferred quite a bit of the family wealth with them when they married. Whether they remained with their family and the husband joined them — matrilocal arrangement — or followed the patrilocal tradition, they acquire servants and animals, which are the tokens of their material worth. There is no doubt that economic factors determined the feasibility of a marriage, and only when economic conditions were satisfactory did the men fall in love with their women.

There is one Hebrew matriarch, Leah, with whom a man did not fall in love but who, ironically, turned out to be a prolific mother, giving birth to many sons and a daughter. By having more children than any other woman in the story, Leah left an indelible mark on the whole tradition. Nevertheless, the text minimizes her importance and contribution and assigns the children that she bore to her husband only. They are all referred to as the children of Jacob/Israel rather than the children of Leah.[8] A further diminution in Leah's status results in her identity as Rachel's sister; she thus remains etched in our memory not as a person in her own right but as the sister of a woman who, at least love-wise, was more fortunate than she. Leah's actions betray jealousy and competition, and the fact that she "gives" her maidservant, Zilpah, to Jacob for procreation purposes suggests vulnerability and a deep sense of insecurity. Leah is never portrayed as a barren woman, yet she is forced to act like one because she wishes to be noticed and wants to fit into the circle of "beloved wives." The issue of barrenness is so all-consuming to the women that even their children become aware of it and sometimes react in a very meaningful fashion. Witness Reuben's actions regarding the mandrakes that, ironically, seem to have made only little difference because they ended up in Rachel's possession. In the aftermath of the story of Reuben and the mandrakes, Leah does get pregnant but presumably because she turned to God, not the mandrakes (Gen 30:14–17).

The women do not fall in love the way the men do, and the reason for that cannot be related only to the male point of view, which predominates in the text. Of course, the writers, editors, and redactors were men, more interested and more comfortable in describing a male perspective, but the ideological agenda in which they invested, demanded a playing down of women's emotions. Moreover, when the narrators, who were perfectly able to describe feelings when they saw fit (e.g., the "crying" Jacob, who is so overcome with emotion when he confronts Rachel that he bursts out weeping),[9] depict sentiments, they focus on the men.

Women do not seem to have tender feelings in the text, and they do not "fall in love." Because of the ritualized aspect of courting, only the males have the right to propose marriage and love; it manifests their control, proves that they make the rules, and reaffirms the notion that the women have to succumb to them. When women's emotions are evident, they are associated with jealousy and a fear that if they cannot produce sons they will lose their "beloved" stature. Rachel, who is obsessed with her inability to have children, pathetically implores Jacob about her condition and is rebuked by him quite severely.[10] When her maid's children are born to them, Rachel pronounces vindication. It is especially instructive to listen to her words when Bilhah's second son is delivered: "I have struggled mightily [Elohim's struggle] with my sister and triumphed . . ." (30:8). Rachel underscores the importance of pregnancy and progeny, without which even the most beautiful, beloved wife cannot maintain her position in the household. Sadly, Rachel's proclamation is also a testimony to the competitive nature of the matrimonial bonds, where a woman's value is determined mainly by her reproductive capacity.[11]

In order for a woman to be fallen in love with, the woman has to leave home (the interior), go outside, and do something useful, for example, help out with the flock or welcome guests to the house. Thus, Rebekah greets Abraham's messenger on behalf of Isaac, and Rachel goes out to meet Jacob. Rebekah's final destination is with Isaac in his home (patrilocal), whereas Jacob stays with his father-in-law for a very long time before he decides to leave and establish his own household in Canaan. When the women acquire the position of "wives," they are expected to stay within the house, take care of the children, and perform other unspecified household chores. Very rarely does a woman in Genesis "go out" after she is married.[12] When the women complete the process of "exposure," they withdraw into a closed world of womanly interior images where males do not seem to be comfortable. Thus, Jacob is irritated with his beloved Rachel when she asks him for children (30:2) and he responds emotionally. Jacob's various frustrations notwithstanding, that outburst insinuates deep discomfort with an area where he is not in control. Likewise, when Leah confronts her husband after the highly charged encounter with Rachel, he simply follows her wishes, showing no particular preference (30:14–16). The periodic bickering between the sisters in the Jacob household is a tribute to the success of a male agenda, which pitted one woman against another on the basis of sexuality and fertility.

The picture that emerges from the aftermath of "love" between men and women is of two separate worlds that are clearly drawn and do not easily merge. The men's portion is more public, and the role of the women is more shadowy. Not only are women supposed to be hidden from public inspection; they must also place all of their prospects in the hands of men. Further, the men in these stories seem to have very little contact with their spouses (beloved or not), nor do they seem to show any interest in the happenings within "the tent." They do have preferences when the issue of favorite sons is raised—which is only natural in the context of Genesis. Almost always, the men's favorite sons are not the same as their wives' favorites: the males seem to appreciate more their firstborns, echoing patrilineal values, whereas the women prefer the younger children—and, as a tribute to women's power in the text, the younger children always prevail.

Dinah is the only sister in Genesis who has apparently come of age; she is not a shepherdess and has stayed in the house, perhaps for too long. Possibly she decides to break away because she feels that she is ripe and that her time has come. Even though the tale does not occur in the familiar Haran environment where Rebekah and Rachel functioned, where the courting ritual was well defined, and where, on a more practical level and as a matter of routine, it was crucial to go out and water the flock, Dinah's general environment is similar to theirs. Admittedly, there is some insecurity among the Jacobites, who are relatively new in Canaan and who cannot fully settle down and acquire land yet, but the text is clear in asserting that Jacob returned to Canaan on a permanent basis. One can argue that because of the temporary haziness of their status, the women, especially those who were eligible and ready for a family of their own, were kept in the house till Jacob's position became clearer. But Dinah, who is a teenager[13] eager to have a taste of the outside world, wishes to "see the daughters of the land." The brothers are said to be out and about attempting to establish a culture, a home, a framework in which to operate coherently (34:5); Dinah may want to do the same. But ideological considerations stemming from the redactors' firm conviction that Jewish survival depended on and could be achieved only by shunning the Canaanites and confirming Yahweh's exclusivity doomed Dinah's excursion from the outset.

The Well and the Virgin

The Men's Search

The stories of the courtship of Rebekah and Rachel are so similar that in some instances they seem to be needlessly repetitive. The Eliezer–Rebekah encounter is recapitulated in a wish–fulfillment sequence as well as in the mode of reality, and commentators have already analyzed some of the reasons behind the duplications.[14] The impression the reader is ultimately left with is of a polished ceremonial dance performed in order to assure the continuity of the family. By the time the stories reach their conclusion, we are intimately familiar with the steps that must be taken to accomplish what the heroes do; we do not necessarily know the characters better — that in itself is not important — but we become familiar with the process that assures the tribe's continuity. In other words, the text emphasizes a few important rites that must be performed before a union between a man and a woman takes place: namely, the man is obliged to seize the initiative; he has to be of the same general background and environment as the bride, preferably the same family; and he is also required to have a substantial amount of material goods to show to the woman's family. The woman has to be a virgin, beautiful, able-bodied, and hospitable. She is required to have features that will attract the man on a more immediate, physical level as well as qualities that hint at the not-so-obvious. For example, Rebekah played the role of a perfect hostess: she offered water not only to Eliezer but to his camels as well; not only did she help out by the well but she invited him to stay with her family as a guest with no strings attached. These steps clearly presented the sister of Laban as compassionate, efficient, and ready to serve. When the ritual is as clear and as focused as these narratives suggest, it is not always necessary to engage the groom in the courting. Anybody who is trustworthy and familiar with the protocol can obtain the right woman for the right man. In fact, when Jacob met Rachel, love may have interfered with his initial judgment, and perhaps because of that, he failed to secure her immediately for himself.

Jacob is portrayed as being much more rash than Eliezer, and even though he takes some essential steps toward recognizing his bride-to-be, he is not cautious enough. He also is out-maneuvered by Laban, who is the master of deception and teaches his son-in-law-to-be a lesson he will never forget. Not only does Laban dispose of his daughters, who were of marriageable age, but he succeeds in putting Jacob on the defensive, thus paralyzing him. In a most canny statement, Laban reminds Jacob that it is the custom in their place to take care of the older daughter before the younger and that if Jacob wants Rachel he will have to work for her as hard as he did for Leah. (Jacob thought, at the time, that he was working for Rachel.) Laban, the greedy villain of Genesis, instructs Jacob in a most profound manner: he inflicts on him an emotional wound and strips him of any capacity to respond in kind. Not only does Laban deceive him as openly as one can (there is a very elaborate wedding feast, at the culmination of which the groom is intimately acquainted with the bride), but it takes Jacob a whole night to find out about the deception. Since the marriage is consummated and the virgin deflowered, Jacob must accept Leah as his. On a purely literary level, the narrators seem to "rebuke" Jacob for his role as the younger brother who deceived Esau in just as ceremonial a manner — except that in the case of Isaac's blessing, Jacob was wearing Esau's clothes and the blind father, though suspicious, was helpless. Moreover, Jacob's deception of his father occurs within the tent, in a discreetly private environment. When Laban gives Leah away, he prepares a very public feast and veils the bride, both of which are socially acceptable customs. The irony of the narrative is that even though Laban is public, Jacob is still trapped.

Both these stories, as repetitive as they are, point to a highly structured society conducting the business of family continuity in a precise fashion. Those who participate know the rules and follow them carefully because their lives depend on them. Any deviation from the norm produces anxiety, suspicion, and finally outright failure. Even when Laban justified his "betrayal" to Jacob, he used the language of custom and ceremony, saying: "it is not thus done (it is not our custom) in our place, to give the younger before the older" (29:26). Indeed, custom played an important role in the process because it harmonized and regulated people's behavior and especially because it left the power brokers' base intact.

Nonetheless, although the courting of Rebekah and Rachel is accomplished within a highly civilized framework where the participants know what to do and how to behave, and although both women belong to a clearly stratified society, the two men that they marry seem to be heading in a new and uncertain direction. As it turned out, the males' movement away from Mesopotamia caused the women ultimately to lose more than the men.[15]

The Symbols of Betrothal

There are specific symbols related to the ritual of securing a bride; almost all of them can be found in the vicinity of the well. Water symbolism, related to life and renewal, can be identified in various other stories in Genesis. The Garden of Eden is filled with waters running from various rivers and rivulets. The waters of the flood, while destroying the wicked, also cleanse and purge those who survive the devastation. Ishmael is saved in the scorching heat of the desert when his mother finds well water (21:19). The angel of Yahweh appears to Hagar, when she first flees her mistress, by a well in the desert (16:7, 14). There is an elaborate "war of the wells" which includes a confrontation between Isaac and the Philistines and a reiteration of the terms of the covenant between Yahweh and the patriarch (chap. 26); in that incident matters of power and land are disputed and the text clearly maintains that Isaac can survive wherever he settles only if he finds "a living well of water" (26:19). Indeed, the Genesis stories are influenced by the desert setting, in which no one can survive without water. The well thus evolves into the symbol of the civilization that depends on it for physical survival and renewal as well as for social adaptability and entrenchment. Water rituals signify adaptation and intimacy, and only those who legitimately "belong" to the well—that is, those who dig it and are recognized as such by naming it[16] —can partake of the daily rituals associated with it.

Rebekah is assigned the task of drawing water from the well that served the needs of her family and friends. She goes to the well, which is also the hub of social action, and there she meets her future husband. The damsel with the pitcher on her shoulder, approaching the water cistern at the end of the day (24:15), is also the woman who thus announces to the man that she is available. The jug properly manifests the young woman's ability to sustain pregnancy and a family of her own. In an unusually elaborate depiction, the narrators tell us the following: ". . . And Rebekah went out, who was born to Bethuel . . . and her bucket on her shoulder. And the girl was very good-looking, a virgin whom no man knew. And she descended to the well and filled her bucket and ascended [or emerged]" (24:15b–16). Rebekah "went out" of her house, carrying the appropriate gadgets, at the right time (evening) and to the right place (the well). The woman's portrait is as complete as it can be, and when Abraham's slave observes her, he knows that he had accomplished for his master most of what he was sent to do.

The meeting between Jacob and Rachel is a variation on the theme of "virgin by the well." Rachel is the shepherdess who brings her father's flocks to the well at midday ("when the day is big," 29:7). Jacob is the flashy, strong suitor who "as soon as he saw Rachel . . . removed the rock from the top (literally, "lip") of the well and watered [to be associated with *wayyiššaq*, "kissed," in v. 11] the flock of Laban, his mother's brother" (29:10). On the face of it, the whole setting of Jacob's pursuit, which emphasizes his physical prowess, belies his earlier representation in the text as "a whole (righteous) man, sitting in tents," in contrast to Esau, who "knows hunting and is a man of the field" (25:27). But while Jacob sits in the "tent," protected and "loved" by his mother, he learns some important lessons that are unraveled when he finally meets his beloved. Not only is Jacob aware of the familial intricacies of success and prosperity; he is deceptively strong and capable of handling difficult chores that sometimes demand the attention of several men. He is also a man who dreams of power and stability in Canaan (28:13–15). But, above all, Jacob is a man of wheeling and dealing, who can shrewdly and quickly assess his prospects. In Laban he found his superior, but Jacob does have the final say and, when the time is right, leaves his father-in-law triumphantly (though in stealth) in order to return to Canaan.

The Breach of Ritual by Dinah

The stage is thus set for the story of Dinah (chap. 34). She is in the position of Rebekah and Rachel before their marriage commitments were made: she is a virgin and — unlike Rachel, who is the younger daughter in Laban's house — the only daughter named in Jacob's household. One of the most jarring ingredients in the narrative — namely, that Dinah is the daughter of Leah (as opposed to Rachel, who was the beloved wife) — proves to be quite ominous, especially since there is little information about the mothers of Rebekah and Rachel. The most striking point of divergence among the three narratives is the environments in which they take place. Rebekah's and Rachel's betrothal commitments were made in Haran, or its close vicinity, whereas Dinah's terrain is Canaan. That difference is crucial, because Jacob and his family are described as having arrived from another locality, not being quite settled in the new land. Moreover, entry into Canaan was associated with danger and trouble for Jacob, who originally fled it because of deceit and fear for his life (27:41–45). Still later he had to fight a deity (32:25) before confronting his brother, who, the text intimates, was very comfortable in the Canaanite environment.

Another difference between the first two stories and Dinah's is the relationship between the males of the house and the woman who was the potential bride. In the stories of Rebekah and Rachel, the two women had some affinity with the men (brothers and father), but there is no hint of closeness in Dinah's relationship with Jacob or her brothers. In fact, whatever association can be inferred from the text is alienation and noncommunication. Jacob does not seem to be interested in his daughter, and whether she loves him and wishes to have a relationship with him or not is not an issue in the narrative. On the other hand, one can draw positive conclusions from some of the negative circumstances described in the text; for example, Dinah, who was at the marriageable age, had not been offered to any prospective groom by her family; neither did anyone come to seek her hand in marriage. She may have decided to act independently so as not to remain a matchless spinster for the rest of her life. We know from other stories in Genesis that women were often troubled about their future; sometimes they even took extraordinary measures in order to secure for themselves a name and a family (e.g., Tamar in chap. 38). Since the text does not suggest that Dinah was involved in treachery or manipulation, we must conclude that the main obstacle to her marrying was environmental. From what the text does say about Jacob — and particularly from his reaction to the brothers' massacre of the Hivites — it is evident that he was not confident enough in the new country and therefore may have been wary of establishing a new family.

When Dinah "goes out" she defies everything that the text had already defined and more: she ventures out of the house without a clear male purpose; in fact, she goes out with the intention of "seeing the women of the land," not to water the flocks or wait for a man to offer her jewels and the hand of his master's son. But, ironically, what does happen to her is what happened to the other women. She thus fits, at least externally and superficially, into the tradition of the woman who goes out of the house, meets the right person who then proceeds to offer her either his master's or his own hand in marriage. But there is a tangle in the Dinah narrative which insinuates that because she goes out on her own — that is, either without permission or without anyone knowing about it — she is first raped and only afterward pursued by her rapist. There is a further twist: Dinah does not meet the "right" man; she meets Shechem, the son of Hamor, who is a local Hivite chieftain who has no blood or other bond with the Hebrews. The chapter goes on to emphasize Shechem's remoteness from the tradition of the Hebrews by describing him, his family, the men of his village, and the rest of the tribe as being uncircumcised, that is, ritually unfit for association with the Hebrews. In glaring contrast to the other betrothal narratives and in a most unsettling manner, Dinah apparently lingers in the house of her rapist before her family reaches any agreement with the family of Shechem. Stated differently, Dinah performs a socially unacceptable act by moving to her rapist/suitor's home before the courting ritual is consummated. Relocating to the house of a suitor was a symbolic assertion as well as a real statement of intent. Dinah violates both the symbolic and the real impact of ritualistic courtship. Because of that breach, she must be restrained.

Inside the Tent

Rebekah and Rachel in the Tent

The story of Isaac's betrothal to Rebekah is, ironically, not his story; furthermore, it is told in detail more than once — all from Eliezer's point of view and each time addressing a different audience. When the narrators finally bring Isaac into the picture, they describe him as noticing the beautiful Rebekah "falling off her camel" (24:64); that is, he observes her performing a ritualized act of obedience to him, her future husband. To complete that ritual she also puts a veil on her face. All Isaac has to do, at that point in the narrative, is to "bring Rebekah into his mother's tent" and love her (24:66–67).

Although continuity is preserved by assuring that the right woman (Rebekah) replaces the deceased mother (Sarah), the issue of the woman's security within and without the tent is just as important — if not more so. When Rebekah completes her journey to Isaac by falling off the camel, she thus acknowledges that the world outside is fraught with risk. But the veil and the fall, though symbols of chastity and submission, are also images of anxiety: the veil implies a deliberate retreat, and falling off a camel suggests a basic weakness that calls for protection. When Rebekah enters Isaac's tent, she is closing the door on the rest of the world and accepting his shelter. Along with that shield, the woman is now ready to accept the love of her husband. The narrators assigned love to men only.[17] Since they are the source of power and love of women is one of the implements of their authority, they transfer their loved one to a place they consider safe (for her as well as for them).

There is an additional incongruity in the marriage to the "right" woman which, strangely enough, evolves into a quasi ritual: the woman who is chosen to be the beloved wife is barren or, at the very least, has great difficulty in achieving pregnancy. Barrenness, which is discovered only when the woman is safely within the confines of her husband's tent, allows the various narratives to describe emotional distress on the part of the women and in most cases brings out the worst in their character. It is also a power tool with which the men manipulate the women: Rachel quarrels with Jacob, who becomes extremely impatient with her crankiness, "and Jacob was angry with Rachel, saying: 'Am I Elohim who prevents you from being fruitful?'" (30:2). This statement further betrays the central issue in all of these "romances" and marriages, namely, the concern with male power and control. When Rachel approaches Jacob she expects a resolution to her problem: "Let me have children," she says. His response ("Am I God?") is in terms of power symbols (Elohim). Rachel, now in the tent, is left to her own devices knowing full well that she has no recourse to the outside world except through her husband. While Rachel succumbs to Jacob's authority, in her hour of need when she passionately pleads with him, he scolds her. On the other hand, when she offers him her maidservant, thus resorting to a solution from within the tent, he gladly accepts. But the reaction from within the tent does not necessarily mean more fulfillment for the woman.[18]

Dinah in the Tent

Like her predecessors, Dinah can be found in the tent too. Although the text does not dwell on how she gets into Shechem's home, it implies that her presence there is highly irregular because not only is Dinah not yet promised to Shechem but she stays with him while the courtship takes place in the house of her father and brothers. The contrast between the environment of the tent in the other betrothal narratives and in the tale of Dinah's rape, courtship, and tent security is quite dramatic. The narrators' purpose in emphasizing violence rather than love and tranquillity in the narrative of Dinah is deliberate. Placing Dinah in her rapist's home while he conducts the ritual of courtship raises fundamental questions about social and familial order. Further, the redactors — on their own or with the help of a narrator who first introduced the story into the tradition — manage to contrive a scene in which they plant false expectations so as to blur the moral and the ritualistic issues. Hence, there may not be anything fundamentally or morally wrong with a woman's going out of her father's house, but something is ritually and socially wrong when she decides to go "see the daughters of the land" rather than "to the cistern." By the same token, there is nothing out of the ordinary in a man "seeing" a woman the way Shechem did, but it is quite another matter if he rapes her and then falls in love with her. Actually, the combination of occurrences, rape and love, muddles the moral issues and casts Shechem in the role of villain/lover. In other words, Shechem the rapist is obnoxious, but Shechem the lover atones right away for committing an obscenity. Finally, we already know from the other narratives that there is nothing inherently wrong in entering a husband's tent, but only after the marriage feast takes place, not while the groom-to-be is still negotiating the conjugal terms. No wonder that when the slaughter of the Hivites takes place, we are not totally comfortable, but neither are we absolutely certain that it is wrong. The narrators succeed in shaking moral certainties by describing ambiguous happenings. Familiar rituals are performed (e.g., the bride is pursued by the groom), but the order of their performance is wrong. A man wants to get married, but he does not follow the assigned script. And if the redactors' point of view is to prevail, it is essential that they draw attention to both the rape and the rapist's lack of circumcision. Shechem is thus portrayed as a disorderly "stranger" who is incapable of functioning in a Hebraic environment because he is not privy to two of its fundamental rituals—namely, taking a bride while she is still pure (associated with water imagery) and virginal and being himself in a pure, ritualized condition (circumcised). The heart of the story is henceforth transferred from the inadequate acts of the woman to the shameful deed of the man.

But the redactors' triumph is in their irrevocable ability to so manipulate the actions and the characters that both Shechem and Dinah emerge negatively. In the final analysis, the narrators imply that she had embarked on the wrong journey ("to see the daughters of the land"). Rashi goes so far as to say: "like mother like daughter"[19] and compares Dinah's "outing" with her mother's "going out" to sleep with Jacob after Reuben provides her with the mandrakes (31:16). The narrators' bias against the stranger as well as against women is transformed in the story into a well-argued case for the brothers' violence. By not dwelling on Dinah's motivation, except in a very esoteric and general way (she went out "to see the daughters of the land"), the text implies that there was something secretive and, therefore, wrong with what she did. The very fact that vague phrases with almost cryptic significance are used leads to suspicion and a speculation that the very activity the woman was involved in was probably wrong. The redacted story engineers the transformation of Dinah, not the brothers, into a culprit.

Compared with the slim amount of information about Dinah's actions, and especially about how she arrived in Shechem's home, we are told almost everything about the brothers. Their designs are lucid from the very start. The openness of the males' intentions and actions is in sharp contrast to the vague motivations of the woman in the text, and the more information there is about them, the more she is pushed into a shadowy background which implies guilt. Even Jacob's passivity is deliberately overlooked by the narrators. The brothers totally control the action and do not seem to be concerned with their father's point of view. When Jacob finally does react, he is troubled not by the impact the rape might have had on his daughter but by the effect on the reputation of the whole family. In other words, the community, rather than the single individual, is upheld as the most significant component in a conflict that involved individuals.[20]

Shechem and Dinah in the Tent?

Before laying to rest Jacob's lack of compassion for Dinah, it should be compared with the attitude of Shechem. There is no question that his raping of Dinah was a horrendously immoral act for which he deserved punishment; but in another of the improbable twists and turns of the Dinah narrative, Shechem is heard consoling his victim and "speaking kindly to her" (v. 4a). Since there is no report about how Dinah arrived in Shechem's house, it stands to reason (by reference to the other narratives where the woman reaches the man's "tent") that this particular moment of "kindness," which is essentially protective of the woman, took place at the moment of her arrival at the tent. This positive gesture on the part of Shechem may be a remnant of an earlier story that might have depicted the Canaanites (assuming that these are Hivites and not

Hurrians) in a more favorable light.[21] If the Hivites of the redacted Masoretic Text are indeed the Hurrians of an earlier text, then Dinah's future prospects were quite spectacular, especially if she was "fallen in love with" by a prince. In the present version, Shechem's reaction could be a remnant of male compassion which was meant to be erased by the redactors because of their convictions that women should not be granted empathy, particularly in matters of sex and friendship with strangers.

* * *

The difference between Jacob's and Shechem's attitude to Dinah points to two diametrically opposed points of view. Jacob's indifference to Dinah's fate and his concern for his own reputation are examples of women's dehumanization by men who are heavily concerned with their own egos, status, and possessions. Shechem's tenderness is a reminder of equality that may have been more prevalent in cultures (like the Cannanite or the Hurrian) that embraced the cult of the goddess and allowed women to come and go freely for social as well as ritualistic purposes.

If women fill clear functions, socially as well as ritually, with appropriate roles as priestesses in temples or as active communal contributors, they do not have to find their definitive destiny only within the tent. But if a woman's final goal is the tent, then when she reaches it, she may find herself to be heavily secluded from the rest of the world. Moreover, the seclusion that the tent offers is not necessarily more protective of women; neither does it offer them ultimate security. On the contrary, although the tent is a means of staying away from external, worldly commotion, it offers very little emotional and psychological solace, as we have seen in the case of Rachel and Jacob. As the author of *The Binding of Isaac* proclaimed: "Undoubtedly, the main history of righteous people is their good deeds,"[22] regardless of their gender. One can certainly be "righteous" within the tent, but the social conflicts and the great battles of good and evil which lead people to take "righteous" viewpoints occur outside the tent. There is a certain immobility that settles in when one's horizons are limited to one's immediate surroundings.

At best, women like Rebekah and Rachel could have vicariously partaken of the great debates of their family and clan. Rebekah was the more fortunate because, even though she manipulated Isaac into recognizing her beloved Jacob, she was the only woman in the household and did not have to be pitted against a rival. Rachel was a much more pathetic figure because, from the very beginning, she was used as an instrument in her father's machinations. When she was ambushed by her own body, she was devastated, and, by using her maidservant as surrogate mother, she furthered the males' social arrangement and institutionalized her isolation.

Rebekah and Rachel were the products of a society in transition. While still upholding values of the old tribe, they were slowly moving in a new direction, away from the culture of Mesopotamia and its adherence to multiple gods and goddesses, away from a more strict reliance on the cycle of nature and the seasons, rivers, and water. These women — Rebekah more than Rachel — retain some of the characteristics of individuals who made a difference in the way the family conducted its affairs. Whether they echo a past power base which Genesis does not afford them, or whether these women simply function as people within a society that was in the midst of turmoil and change, they are depicted as desirable, admirable, and as balancing the men of the tribe.

Throughout the ages, the Genesis matriarchs drew praise from rabbis and scholars who upheld them as emblems of a familial ideal which sprouted in Judaism.[23] Even Leah was fully incorporated into the nation's psyche and faith by way of her children, two of whom, Levi and Judah, were directly related to the great kings (David), prophets (Moses), and priests (Aaron) of Israel. In an ironic twist, Rachel evolved into the symbol of the mournful, caring mother who finally found a voice of compassion and shed bitter tears for her lost children. In a great eschatological pronouncement, Jeremiah promises her that, at the end of days, her children will be fully restored (Jer 31:14-16).

Dinah is delineated in Genesis as the product of an environment that was absolutely different from that of Mesopotamia. She lives in Canaan and has to adhere to a new set of Hebraic practices, which, though not yet fully articulated, are headed in the way of control and closure. Accordingly, Dinah was not supposed to go out and socialize with Canaanites; she could not accept the offers of a Canaanite prince who wished to marry her because he was not a Hebrew, not a fellow tribesman, not a party to Yahweh's covenant, and not circumcised. Because of the action she took, Dinah lost her voice in the narrative, and the brothers' activities emerged as far more significant and much more decisive than hers. Ironically, the brothers also acquired more possessions when they completed their brutal takeover of the Hivites' village. In a perverse way, they concluded what other brothers before them corroborated, namely, that a woman's "going out" must be invariably linked with material rewards for the males.

Rebekah and Rachel are portrayed in the text as the Hebrew women who accepted personal confinement and tribal exclusivity; Rebekah is even reported to have been concerned that her son not marry a Hittite woman (27:46). Dinah, by comparison, was more willing to associate with her new neighbors; her "going out" was interpreted by the tradition (established by the redactors) as a rebellion for which she was immediately punished. All three women point the way for the rest of the community: accept Yahweh and his covenant and gain access to Canaan; restrict women to their men's tents and gain access to tribal exclusivity; shield women from uncircumcised foreigners and gain power and material goods.

NOTES

1. The patriarchs have children as soon as they sleep with the various maidservants, e.g., Hagar, Bilhah, and Zilpah (see chaps. 16 and 30).

2. This is inevitably associated with the development of gender roles in Hebrew civilization. If one examines the mythology of the Garden of Eden and its social message along patriarchal lines, one is led to believe that not only are women weaker than men, they are also extremely vulnerable and therefore need protection.

3. Poignantly articulated in Judges as well as in the books of Samuel and Kings; see Trible, *Texts of Terror*.

4. There are two versions of the story of Abraham's servant, Eliezer, and Rebekah and her household. The more cryptic version points to the presence of a strong mother figure in the house. On two occasions the text tells us that Rebekah "ran and told these things to her mother's house" (24:28) and later "her brother and mother said: 'Let the girl stay with us for a few, or ten, days and then go.'" In the main part of the text, when negotiations about Rebekah's future take place, the men (presumably Laban and Bethuel) seem to be in charge and they do not consult with her at all. It seems that the males in the household are interested in the material details that Abraham's servant so profusely provides.

5. See the emphasis on water and food imagery for both people and animals, and the use of the camel for transportation, which is typical of the desert. Travelers like Eliezer or Jacob depended on the good offices of hosts and hostesses like Rebekah, Rachel, and Laban, who provided them with the necessities of survival.

6. Rashi maintains, in his commentary on 29:13, that after examining Jacob's body quite closely (hugging and kissing), Laban realized that he had very little (or no) jewelry on him.

7. This happens specifically within the prophetic tradition, where there is a strong sense of matrimonial links that must be realized if the covenant between God and his people is to be binding; see Hosea 1; 3.

8. There is one exception, which further underlines the position of women in that society: Dinah, the only daughter that Leah bore to Jacob, is recognized as her mother's daughter, and that recognition is also her stigma.

9. Abraham too is concerned emotionally about the fate of his son Ishmael, when Sarah decides to banish him and his mother. Abraham shows his concern and tenderness by preparing meticulously for their dangerous journey (21:14).

10. Rabbinic commentators have been particularly unhappy with the response of Jacob, who they felt was mean-spirited and should have been much more patient with Rachel. The RAMBAN (Nachmanides), in a most poignant comment wondering about Jacob's state of mind and psychological equilibrium, finally concludes that indeed Jacob must have prayed to God (as did his father before him when Rebekah was in the same situation) but that God did not respond to him. Jacob's angry reply to Rachel was thus interpreted by the RAMBAN to show frustration rather than sheer anger. In an even more extraordinary approach to the same text, Rabbi Isaac A'rama differentiates between the two "purposes" or natures embodied in the existence of women: one is associated with the word *'iššâ,* "woman," which suggests that she has capacities similar to those of a man (*'iš*), like understanding and wisdom. The other "nature" is related to "Eve," the mother of all living people, which implies that women were assigned the task of perpetuating the race. If a woman cannot bear children she must strengthen her other nature—namely, the rational—and concentrate on righteous activities like male Zaddiqim do. A'rama concludes that Jacob's anger was an attempt to instruct Rachel in the above and that he was particularly concerned that Rachel seemed to have concentrated all of her efforts on one aspect of her being (*The Binding of Isaac* [Jerusalem, 1966] Gate 9, p. 233 [in Hebrew]).

11. Margaret Atwood pursues this point to its frightening absurdity in *The Handmaid's Tale* (New York: Fawcett Crest, 1985). In that novel, the women function only as "vessels," who either can or cannot bear children.

12. No wonder Rashi is condescending toward Leah, who "goes out" to

meet Jacob after the exchange she has with Rachel and Reuben regarding the mandrakes (30:14–16).

13. She is referred to as na'ărâ, "grown girl," and yaldâ, "child."

14. See, e.g., Robert Alter, *The Art of Biblical Narrative* (New York: Basic Books, 1981).

15. See specifically the arguments made by S. J. Teubal regarding the position of priestesses in Mesopotamia and the link to the Hebrew matriarchs (*Sarah the Priestess* [Athens, OH: Swallow Press, 1989]).

16. Names indicate uniqueness as well as association; for example, the wells of Abraham (and Isaac) signify establishment within a geographical locale as well as association with Yahweh, who directs all important acts.

17. When intimacy and love are mentioned in connection with women, it is toward other women (see the daughter of Jephthah [Judges 11]), as if the possibility of a deeper bond for women could have developed only between them.

18. All matriarchs, including the fertile Leah, give their maidservants to their husbands in a bid to acquire more power and status.

19. It is also important to remember that Leah, who is the unloved wife, is the less sympathetic of the two sisters. Moreover, Leah has no voice compared with Rachel, within the narratives as well as within the tradition as a whole.

20. Various scholars have suggested that the role of Jacob in the Dinah matter was, at best, ambiguous; Zakovitch, "Assimilation in Biblical Narratives," in *Empirical Models for Biblical Criticism*, ed. J. H. Tigay (Philadelphia: University of Pennsylvania, 1985).

21. Cuthbert A. Simpson suggests that the original story (which we do not possess) was probably not a rape story and that the rape was introduced in order to score an ideological point, namely, that the Canaanites should not be associated with and that the violation of a woman's virginity should be punishable by death (*The Interpreter's Bible* [New York: Abingdon, 1952] 1:733–37).

22. In Nechama Leibowitz, *Studies in the Book of Genesis* (Jerusalem: Jewish Agency Pub. House, 1987) 233.

23. See some of the legends in L. Ginzberg, *The Legends of the Jews* (Philadelphia: Jewish Publication Society, 1968) 341, where the matriarchs are even invested with prophetic qualities.

4

THE STORY OF DINAH
(GENESIS 34)

Strangers and Canaanites

Gērîm

BEFORE PROCEEDING with a detailed analysis of the Dinah
story, we have to account for the role of "strangers" in the ideology
of the redactors, because it is closely tied to Dinah and to the role
of women in Israelite society. A note of caution is in order here since
the subject of "strangers" is not of a piece in the Hebrew Scriptures.
Neither is it consistently treated in Judaism. On the one hand, there
is a clear statement in Exodus, but not exclusive to that book, that
"any stranger that lives with you and gives thanks to Yahweh during
the Passover ("gives thanks" is translated for the more literal:
"make"), you will circumcise each one of his males. . . . There will
be one Torah (teaching) for the citizen and the stranger in your
midst" (12:48–49). There is even a provision of equality for strangers
in the Sinaitic epiphany (20:11b). In one of the most eloquent statements in the Pentateuch (Exod 22:20) the narrators acknowledge
that the very nature of the Israelite experience in Egypt demands
that they be compassionate to those who are stateless, privilege-less,
and looking for acceptance. More than that, almost every time the
"stranger" is mentioned in Exodus, he is in the company of other
social underdogs, like widows and orphans. Presumably, those to
whom the text refers and those who fit the "stranger" category
during the days of the exodus (or at an earlier time in Hebraic history
and mythology) were ready to proclaim their monotheism, like
modern-day converts who switch religious and social allegiances.
But even when there is no direct reference to conversion, many

sections of the Pentateuch express fundamental compassion for the fate of the stranger and articulate a warning about treating him unfairly.[1]

The "Other Seven" Peoples

Other parts of the Mosaic Law verbalize a different point of view addressed to a different audience with an entirely new perspective.[2] The book of Deuteronomy, which is, ironically, considered by the Jewish tradition to be the greatest of Moses' books (certainly it highlights a significant portion of Moses' career), outlines a political program that fails to account for the stranger and emphasizes instead the corruption and deprivation of "those seven peoples more numerous than you" (Deut 6; 7; 9), who worship other gods and therefore are unworthy of existence. The Canaanites are juxtaposed with Yahweh's "holy nation" (7:6), who must strictly follow the terms of the covenant "cut" with the patriarchs in Genesis. The seven peoples are not offered the privilege of conversion; they are taboo to the Hebrews because of their Canaanite connection. Their "strangeness" is first of all cultural and religious, but, more important, they happen to occupy the same stretch of land that Yahweh "promised" to his chosen people. Political considerations coupled with ideological convictions emphasized the "evil" of Canaan. The dark myth of Noah and his three sons (Gen 9:18–28) acquired significant meaning; Ham's transgression (which landed in Canaan's lap) was familial as well as communal and helped solidify the great mistrust of all those non-Israelites who settled in Canaan.

Recognizing the more extreme faction of the redactors, who fanatically embraced monotheism, is essential for a better understanding of the treatment of "strangers" and Canaanites in Genesis. The triumph of that contingent must be placed within the political framework of expediency. But the key to the redactors' successful bid to polarize the world between "us" and "them" is in some of the more enduring characteristics of monotheism. One of the greatest features of monotheistic worship is its exclusiveness. However, the belief in an absolute God who selects a community for purposes of worshiping and perpetuating a certain life-style is problematic because it can deteriorate into racism, with the "chosen" community holding the banner of privilege and righteousness. Nevertheless, such religious conviction does provide the believer with certainty and peace of mind. The select community is secure wherever it is, knowing that it is watched and directed by God.

Jewish exclusivity, as it was perceived by the Jewish Babylonian community, was aimed against non-Jews in general, and more particularly against "the inhabitants of Canaan," who were perceived as evil because of their different ideology and worship. The redactors' position was a firm, Jewish political viewpoint, and it called for a "return to Zion," which presumably would enable Jews to cultivate their own land, develop their institutions of power and legislation, and worship the supreme Yahweh. Even though universality was implied in the classical prophets' description of the "return,"[3] the redactors played it down and there is no sign of it in Genesis. The latter progresses from universalism (the creation of the cosmos and its first humans) to particularism (Abraham and his clan), emphasizing "specialness" and settlement in the land of Canaan. Eventually, all the non-Hebrews who attempted to settle and occupy Canaan, regardless of their national, political affiliations, were identified with a fundamental evil that had to be eradicated by the chosen community. But, more and more, the destructive process was assigned directly to Yahweh, who responded to the needs of his people and who demanded in return exclusive worship.

We have seen all along that the more extreme redactive, ideological convictions were most clearly manifested in the story of Dinah, where the woman was presented as a rebellious individual who dared to "go out" of her father's house without consulting any of the men. Her story helped to reinforce the idea that women were not trustworthy and required constant watching. In addition, the narrators took a strong stand on the issue of the settlement of Canaan, lending their support to the concept of a "holy war" that, they claimed, sometimes must be fought if a nation is to survive.

In the following analysis, the story of Dinah, the daughter of Leah and Jacob and the sister of Simeon and Levi, will be approached from within its very core as well as from its more specific, redactive point of view. The story is bloody and explosive; the narrators and redactors of Genesis used violence as part of a plan to reduce women to stereotypes of frailty and sexuality. The ideology expounded by the redactors created a chasm between men and women not only with the intention of enslaving and subjugating women, but, paradoxically, for the ultimate purpose of communal and national harmony. It was very clear to the Babylonian redactors that the answer to the depressing state of exile and dispersion was full acceptance of Yahweh and his covenant. The road from there to community and nation was not obscure anymore. In this highly charged political setting, the stranger's role changed so radically that his participation in Jewish national life was ruled out. Like women, the strangers became the scapegoats of a society trying to define and find for itself a place in the universe.

The redacted story of Dinah is of a Hebrew woman who arrived in Canaan, looked for company and friendship, and found a "stranger." The story involves Hebrew men who were not ready to tolerate a stranger in their midst. The violent cloud that surrounds the events of this narrative leaves people gasping and questioning. The redactors did not flinch, though, and their answers were consistently ideological. They focused on Shechem, the uncircumcised stranger whom they converted into a rapist, bold enough to fall in love with the woman he raped. They also highlighted the brothers' violence, which, so they claimed, was provoked by the rape. But, by no coincidence, careless women, strangers, and a stake in Canaan were the major issues of postexilic Judaism as seen in the Ezra-Nehemiah texts as well as in Deuteronomy.[4] Accordingly, the redactors transformed Dinah's misfortune into a warning to women about the dangers that lurk outside of the house and about the importance of tribal integrity and exclusivity.

Who Went Out and Why?

An examination of texts referring to people performing the ritual of "going out" in Genesis yields interesting results because it points not only to women who find husbands for themselves, as we have seen, but also to Cain and Jacob. Cain "goes out" in disgrace after killing his brother, but, curiously, he establishes a family (4:16-17). Jacob "goes out" on an arduous journey that leads him to his God as well as to his future wives. The men's "going out" scenes involve complex journeys which point to a larger social and political agenda. Not only do the males enlarge their horizons and gain material and spiritual benefits from their travels, but, while traveling, they seem to dictate the terms of their existence within the environment. In the

case of Jacob, for example, the landscape itself changes as soon as
he enters it and there is no mistaking his dominance (Gen
28:10–22). Since Dinah is said to "go out" in a very general context
(not expressly in order to meet her future husband), and since she
is not accompanied by the traditional symbols of conjugal pursuit
(e.g., flocks), it could be argued that she may have gone out the way
the men did, namely, with a larger program in mind. But as the
narrative develops she actually seems to be "going out" to find her
familial fortunes. The narrators thus quell any heroic motivation for
"the daughter of Leah." Moreover, in the form in which we have it,
Dinah's "going out" has been interpreted (especially by male commentators), by and large, negatively. The heart of Rashi's interpretation, for example, is the comparison between Dinah's "going out"
and her mother's "going out" toward Jacob. In the latter incident,
as Rashi reminds us, Leah was approaching Jacob in order to claim
what she won from her sister earlier in the day, namely, sex with
Jacob (30:16). Rashi goes on to compare daughter and mother,
claiming that Dinah was up to no good or that she was asking for
sexual trouble. Her "going out" in Rashi's mind was reminiscent of
her mother's "going out" to sleep with her husband. In fact, Rashi
goes so far as to suggest that both of them, but particularly Dinah,
were in the category of *yas'ānît*, "a woman who goes out," a euphem-
ism for whore. Even in some modern commentaries where Dinah
is seen as the victim of the narrative, the emphasis is on the noble
gesture of the brothers, who took revenge in behalf of their sister.[5]

The Daughter of Leah

Why did Dinah leave her father's house? The reason was social,
according to the surface of the text ("to see the daughters of the
land"), but this becomes more complex with further analysis. The
focus here is on a core of interior motivations which cast Dinah in
the role of an active woman who was aware of her tribe's traditions
and, like the other women we have already observed, was intent on
fulfilling them. She was cognizant of her own status as the "daughter
of Leah" (34:1), which meant that she was not the favorite daughter,
just as her mother was the unloved wife. The fact that the text
emphasizes her connection to Leah implies that she knew that she
would not be able to "go out" and find her man the way her aunt,

Rachel, had. Leah, in her time, did not "go out" to the well to greet
Jacob either. She, the eldest daughter of Laban, was forced on Jacob
because she did not have attributes like her sister. The text is careful
to differentiate the various women, particularly the matriarchs, and
Dinah must be placed within the tradition of Leah, a legacy that is
very different from that of Rachel. Accordingly, Dinah cannot sit in
the house and wait for the right man to come along and offer her
his "tent," because her father Jacob is not interested in her the way
he is interested in Joseph, the son of Rachel.

More important, the narrative provides ample evidence that at
this time in Jacob's life, he is not the powerful patriarch of the family
that he may have been in the past. His glory days are over and when
he finally returns to Canaan, he is "crippled" (32:32b) in more than
one way. For better or for worse, when Jacob is transformed in the
text into Israel (32:29) he, ironically, loses some of the qualities that
were associated with him at the beginning of his journey. For
example, whereas Jacob of the past was physically strong (29:10) and
passionate (29:11, 18), ready to work relentlessly (fourteen long
years) for what he considered a prize (Rachel), Jacob of the present
is "silent" when he hears about his daughter's "defilement" (or "pollution") (34:5) and waits for his sons to return from the field before
reacting to what has transpired. Is Jacob shocked? Overwhelmed?
Too tired to respond? Trying to absorb what happened? Or, what
seems to be more consistent with the whole of the text, is he just
weak, uncaring and indifferent to Dinah, the one daughter of his
unattractive wife? Indeed, Jacob's nonreaction bolsters the argument that Dinah had to take matters into her own hands because
her father did not care and, at this point in his life, did not have the
same power that Laban had had when Jacob asked him for Rachel's
hand in marriage.

In many other ways as well, the Jacob household was in disarray.
Reuben, who took an enormous risk as well as quite a bit of liberty
when he slept with Bilhah (35:22), was not immediately rebuked (or
cursed or punished) by the concerned patriarch, who is said to have
"heard" about it. Joseph's tattling about the sons of Bilhah and
Zilpah (37:3) raises the ire of the brothers, who finally take their
revenge, and Joseph's sundry dreams lead even his doting father to
distress. In the case of Reuben, we finally find out that Jacob was
angry and indeed lashed out at his oldest son (49:4), but at the time

the affair takes place, he just "hears" about it and does nothing.

Jacob is undoubtedly the patriarch of the family, but it is a family in turmoil looking for stability in a new land and searching for a power base that will establish their legitimacy. While Reuben undertakes that search by violating his father's bed and Joseph does the same by exaggerating his own appeal, Simeon and Levi approach the challenge with violence, deceit, and cunning not unlike the ploys used by Jacob himself in his younger days.

"Going out" thus becomes a rallying phrase used in the text to signify belonging, security, and community. Rebekah and Rachel "go out" of their home because they belong in their community and are looking forward to continuing that association. Dinah "goes out" because she belongs only marginally and is not yet part of a cohesive community. At the opening stages of chap. 34, she is ready to break away from her family, if only temporarily, and is looking to find a new assembly of people, "the women of the land," who, she hopes, will embrace her and make her feel more secure and at home.

When Shechem enters the story, he is characterized as "seeing her" (v. 2a), which correlates with Dinah's goal — "to see" and seek new relationships. As soon as Shechem appears on the scene, he responds to Dinah's yearning for community, maybe even a family. At first glance, he is not very different from Isaac, who "lifted up his eyes and saw" Rebekah falling off a camel (23:63); Isaac then recognized her as his bride. Nor is Shechem's "sighting" of Dinah different from Jacob's "seeing" the beautiful Rachel (29:10).

Indeed, the use of the term "seeing" to invoke love (as well as lust) is pervasive in Genesis. The woman in the garden first "saw" that the fruit was "lovely to eat" and that recognition led to sexual understanding. Moreover, Isaac and Jacob fall in love with Rebekah and Rachel, respectively, after "glancing at" (or "seeing") them. Hence, the narrated order of events in the Dinah story is quite shocking, if not incredible: the story moves from "he saw" to "he took her and lay with her and tortured her" (v. 2b). This particular sequence recalls a different tale, which is indeed the tale of a rapist/prince (Amnon) who lusts for a woman, lures her into his room, and rapes her (Tamar). But the climax (or anticlimax) of that affair occurs after Amnon rapes Tamar, when he literally discards her and "hates her" more than he ever loved her. Shechem does not lure the woman, neither does he lust for her. When Dinah's narrators carry on with her story, they tell us that, unlike the other rapist (Amnon), this one (Shechem) "cleaves" to the rape's subject (v. 3). Not only does this order of events plainly suggest that the authors are presenting a redacted version of the tale, but it intimates that there is a reason, ideological or otherwise, for the redaction.

But even with this in mind, the personality of Shechem, as it is projected in the few words he utters to Dinah, emerges as sympathetic. When the text pronounces: "And his soul cleaved to Dinah, the daughter of Jacob, and he loved the girl and he spoke to her dearly" (spoke to her heart) (v. 3) it expresses in tender terms the love that Shechem felt for Dinah. By comparison with the other stories of "falling in love," the impression is that this one too was immediate and passionate. The story of Shechem's love is related to two urgent issues that Dinah faced and that the other beloved women did not. The first is her status in Jacob's house; Shechem, for the first and only time in the story, legitimizes her as "the daughter of Jacob." In the context of Genesis, where one had to belong to a father more than to a mother, this must have been music to Dinah's ears. The second issue was speech. The ability to communicate and the phenomenon of dialogue are central to an understanding of both the text's characters and the redactors' purpose.[6] On this particular level, the only genuine speech in the story is attributed to Shechem; he is kind and loving (albeit after manifesting cruelty and a lack of sensitivity) whereas all the others are deceitful.

Speech and Cleaving

The sometimes cryptic aspect of speech in the text is a sign of redaction and editorial manipulation, but it also marks action and deeds rather than theoretical speculations. Speech, together with its correlatives, is one of the most important elements in the whole of the Hebraic tradition — particularly divine speech, which guides people and advises them of their destiny.[7]

Speech in Jacob's household denotes union, as when he summons his wives, Rachel and Leah, about departure from Laban's home (31:4–16); it also connotes deception, as the various Jacob–Laban encounters exhibit. At very important points in the patriarchs' journeys, God seems to interfere and "speak" to them, particularly about the covenant (28:13–15). When Shechem speaks to Dinah, he recognizes her as a person of value. As in the other love episodes, here too the man does more than just fall in love with the woman; he invariably says something to her that correlates with the act of falling in love.

Indeed, speaking to a person, beloved or not, is a sign of recognition as well as a measure of respect and equality. In the Dinah narrative, the combination of "cleaving," "loving," and "speaking" places Shechem in the tradition of the Garden of Eden, where the narrators explicitly maintain that: "This is why a man should leave his father and his mother and cleave to his woman (wife) and they will be one flesh" (2:24). The context of the exhortation, which comes on the heels of the creation of the woman from the man's flesh, provides for maximum intimacy, physical and spiritual, between a man and a woman and underscores their equality.[8] It is more than revealing to note that at no time do the Hebrew patriarchs "cleave" to their wives or to other women.

Shechem's "cleaving" to Dinah might suggest (by comparison with the Eden text) that there was a sexual encounter between the two before the courting ritual was undertaken by Shechem's family. Further, if there was a question about Dinah's participation in the "rendezvous," it might be answered by referring to her youth and innocence, coupled with her awe of the person who was said to be "the most respected of all in the house of his father" (v. 19b). But the more attractive interpretation places the young woman within the limits of power and worth. Dinah, no doubt, would have used her sexuality to cement further the union between her and Shechem (Tamar does it in another context in chap. 38). She is ready to stay with him, which further aggravates the brothers, who, at the peak of the slaughter, "take Dinah out of the house of Shechem" (v. 26b). Only then do "they go out." When Dinah "goes out," it is for friendship and dialogue; when they "go out" it is with blood on their hands.

"Going Out" toward Disaster and Silence

Dinah's act of "going out," which promised to be of some significance to her and which placed her within an active framework of initiative and responsibility, loses momentum when the rape occurs. Shechem's (redacted) act thus casts a cloud not only on him but on the raped woman too. Since the smooth narrative falters somewhat with the insertion of the violent act, and since this disruption inflicts a wound on Dinah's and Shechem's motivations, the suggestion that the redactors' purpose was indeed to poison the readers' impressions of the young woman and her "prince" is more than validated. Further, as soon as the rape takes place, the active woman becomes completely passive. Not only does Shechem's reported act manage to violate her integrity as a free woman, but henceforth, she is robbed of a voice (as well as action). This is the major reason for the brothers' intrusion, and by implication, the main reason for embracing the voice of the narrators, who obscure as much as they can the character of the initial heroine of the tale and focus instead on the brothers and their revenge.

Dinah's silence makes room for the pronouncement of ideological convictions stemming from the redactors' dark landscape of survival at all costs. When they introduce the rape into the story, the redactors punish the woman simply because she transgressed the command "you shall not interact or marry them" (Deut 7:3). They thus use the story of Dinah, emphasizing her "going out," as a lesson that demonstrates their agreement with the Deuteronomistic doctrine and as a yardstick for her viability as a person with a voice and an identity.

We have suggested thus far that in the redacted story, the main act of violence intimately related to Dinah's "going out," the rape, was presented by the redactors as a two-edged sword. First, since she left her father's house she signaled that she was a worthless woman. As a result, whatever happened to her in the wake of leaving was predicated on that act; moreover, in that instance, the "going out," Dinah was looking to be raped. Second, and more important, Dinah's action of leaving the security of her father's house was ideologically disastrous, and she was instantly punished for it by being raped. In the first case, though Dinah is still perceived to be a functioning member of the Jacob family, she is being condemned because she stepped out of the family line. In the second circumstance, she is looked down upon from the very start because she rebels and attempts to do precisely what the strict theodicy, articulated by the Deuteronomists and their adherents, tells the nation not to do. In that context, her socializing effort is not just a mistake but an outright sin for which she has to be punished. The difference between the two approaches lies in the emphasis: whereas the first interpretation views the affair from a personal-familial perspective, the second places it within a broad, national context. In the latter, Dinah becomes a symbol for the whole community, and, through her, Israelite/Jewish women are warned to stay within the fold and not attempt any kind of union — least of all a sexual/religious one — with the Canaanites.

Hamor, the Hivite

Hamor, the father of Shechem, "goes out" to speak to Jacob about his son's desire with regard to Dinah (v. 6). He ultimately approaches the brothers as well, in a conciliatory tone which promises inclusion and cooperation (vv. 8-10). Hamor's attitude is similar to that of his son, specifically when the latter, who presumably raped Dinah, "cleaved and spoke kindly to her." We have just argued that loving, cleaving, and speaking to a woman one has just raped are not common happenings, and the fact that the narrative presents this order of events testifies to its redaction. Whereas Shechem seems to pursue a personal (bordering on the intimate) appeal to Dinah, Hamor's personal and general entreaty to the Jacobites is ultimately a political statement that seeks accommodation and inclusion: "And intermarry with us . . . and settle among us and the land will be before you; live and trade within it and settle it (hold on to it)" (vv. 9-10) It is thus no accident that when Jacob's reaction to the whole affair is finally registered in the narrative, it is a political one as well. Jacob, who seeks to be a "citizen" of Canaan, realizes that his best strategy, at this point in his sojourn, is peaceful rapprochement. The economic/political argument continues to dominate the affair when Hamor and Shechem return to their people and present before them Jacob's sons' "conditions." In fact, nothing is said about Shechem's wish to marry Dinah; rather, the focus of the report is "let them settle in the land . . . which is very spacious . . ." (v. 21).[9] Hamor goes so far as to maintain that the Hivites will gain from associating with the Israelites, thus becoming "one people" (v. 22) with them.

Dinah and the Hivites in a Contemporary "Midrashic" Perspective

We have viewed the incident of Dinah's "going out" from two different points of view, one adhering to the literal account in

Genesis and the other considering the redactors of the story. Attention to the latter placed the event within a "midrashic" perspective.[10] Since the redactors of the text were involved in a task that was essentially interpretative as well as creative, they are a part of the midrashic process that became more influential as the Scriptures were canonized. Renée Bloch states that "the canonizing of Scripture was of the greatest importance for the genesis of the midrashic genre."[11] The overt as well as the hidden assumption behind the midrashic phenomenon was that the word of God was revealed at a certain point in history, but that it was addressed to everyone at all times. That is why the words of God must stay infinitely open to all generations who wish to find new meanings in the divine message. That is why God's words must be subject to different nuances that invariably crop up in a new age and in a different environment. As Bloch further suggested, the midrash is bound to a text but does not stop with the text. Midrash is also "the open word, the open door, through which we are always just passing."[12] Ultimately, by resorting to the methods of midrashic exegesis, we not only extract the "relevancy" of any particular text, but we create a new text which further illuminates the old text but also has a life of its own. The midrashic method is clearly comparative and intertextual. The redactors, in their function as exegetes used a variety of texts in order to create their own midrash on Dinah. The most weighty text at their disposal was the Amnon and Tamar story, which dealt with the same topic, and included not only personal elements but political ones as well. After all, the main protagonists and antagonists of that story were affiliated with the royal family; as a subtext, avenging the rape of Tamar was also an instance of the struggle for political power between the various brothers/princes of the realm.

In their attempts to politicize the story of Dinah, her brothers, and the Hivites, the redactors midrashically inserted some new elements and episodes and excised others. One such midrashic element was the rape itself. In the commentary provided in this study, which in its own way is "midrashic," we ascertain that Dinah's "going out" should be divorced from the rape. The story, from our own perspective, is that of innocent love between two young people who were ready to merge culturally, politically, and religiously, and we have tried to make the case for it. Accordingly, Dinah and

Shechem must be seen as a man and a woman who accidently met and, in a rather romantic vein (not too different from Romeo and Juliet), committed themselves to each other.

Placing the issue of "going out" in a midrashic framework will answer the question about why the heroine went out, and the proposed answer will first be that Dinah went out in an attempt to socialize. As to the question of why she directed her efforts at the Canaanites (rather than other Hebrews), there are not yet sufficient answers. In order to respond to these issues we focus on two circumstances: (1) Since the Jacobites are portrayed in this narrative as newly arrived in the land, it is quite possible that their links with other Hebrews who had already settled in Canaan or were in the process of doing so, were not strong enough. Therefore the Jacobites may not have been aware of other eligible Hebrew males who might have been interested in Dinah. (2) Dinah's future prospects were not the top priority in Jacob's dwelling because of her position in the household as "the daughter of Leah," the unloved wife. Moreover, it is not unreasonable to suspect that Dinah was aware of her condition, felt alone and abandoned, and took a stand that ultimately shocked her family. The text does not fail to remind us that Dinah was Leah's daughter, and daughters sometimes reenact important events in the lives of their mothers. Dinah's "going out" could have been the enactment of a ritual that her mother never fulfilled, and in that sense the daughter vindicated (not imitated as Rashi interprets) the mother, who at the time of her marriage was given to her husband under "veiled" pretenses. More precisely, Dinah's act as an attempt to skirt her mother's fate is, above all, a public act, contrary to the sneaky move of Laban, who forced Leah into Jacob's bed. The most compelling contrast is Shechem's falling in love with Dinah; Leah was never loved or desired by her husband. When Shechem professes his love to Dinah, she becomes, for one moment in her life, the beloved woman experiencing emotions that only the major matriarchs of the text (excluding her own mother) must have experienced before her. Ironically, since the limited panorama of the courtship in Genesis allows Dinah to take at least the first step toward her future husband, she accomplishes her initial mission. Her deviation from the norms of the text occurs when she takes the second step and extends a social invitation to the Canaanites; to accomplish that, the heroine had to go to the temple of the goddess.[13]

At this exact point in the action, the redactors intervene and steer the story away from a happy ending. They focus on one of the leading verbs in the chapter, "to see," and use it against the woman. Hence, she goes out "to see" the Canaanites and is indeed "seen" by Shechem, who immediately "takes her, lies with her and tortures [rapes] her" (v. 2). The redactors thus warn from the very start that even if Dinah meant no harm, even if she left the house innocently, she was destined to be violated because of the very nature of the corrupt Canaanites and the "peoples" affiliated with them. When the woman and the stranger meet, the narrators claim, disaster strikes.

But without the redactive "rape" commentary, the incontrovertible linguistic evidence is that both Dinah and the Hivites she confronts aspire to a merger that will go beyond the personal bond between the young couple (vv. 9-10, 21-22). In that sense, when Dinah and Hamor "go out," they are looking for expansion and inclusion. The latter concepts were absolutely anathema to the redactors, who manipulated the text so as to present Dinah as a rebel.

We have already seen that the redactive postexilic climate was strongly slanted against goddess worship and womanly corruption, both of which, so the ideologues argued, were connected and had to be uprooted. Because the redactors accepted all the basic tenets of the classical prophets' ideology, they articulated an antigoddess, anti-Canaanite point of view. Dinah was thus condemned by them before she ever encountered her rapist/prince because she dared to go out of her father's house to socialize with a segment of the population with whom postexilic Jews believed they should not have socialized. Thus, when the rape occurs in the text, it functions as a crime and a punishment, both of which are immediately perpetrated on the woman for reasons that make sense only within the redacted version.

The Brothers "Go Out"

The third reference to "going out" in the story is associated with the brothers' intentional demand of the Hivites for circumcision. This initiates a storm of violence at the end of which they take their sister out of Shechem's house and "go out" (v. 27b). Circumcision gives the story a specific Yahwistic flavor, which brings to mind the Abrahamic covenant. But it also underscores Dinah's "going out" as an aberrant act. Unlike Abraham, for example, who leaves his home in Haran at Yahweh's command, Dinah is not told by Yahweh to leave. Unlike Rebekah and Isaac, who send Jacob out of their home in order to find a wife outside of Canaan (they typically do not like the Canaanite women), Dinah leaves her house precisely in order to find company among the Canaanites. Dinah's story is thus a total reversal of the stories of the patriarchs, and it concludes in the reverse as well: while they are successful, she fails miserably. Her act, in the redactive Yahwistic realm, was neither careful nor in line with the covenantal promise because she went out to assimilate into the Canaanite environment, not to claim it as her own, as the covenant dictated. Simeon and Levi try to alleviate her "sin" by finally "saving" her from her rapist; their "going out" is decisive both for Dinah and the Hivites. After what happens to the village and the villagers, it will be difficult, if not impossible, for anyone to follow Dinah's footsteps. Stated differently, when the brothers "go out," they slam the door in the face of the Hivites and at the same time diminish Dinah's freedom to choose her associates and establish a home of her own.

In many ways, the plot to "deceive," exclude, and kill the Hivites serves as punishment and as crime. While the brothers rightly penalize the perpetrator of the rape (both crimes, rape and circumcision, are associated with a sexual kind of violation), they do not administer the punishment fairly. After all, even within the confines of the tale the whole tribe was not involved in Shechem's affair. When Jacob finds out what actually transpired, even he is shocked.[14] But on another level, circumcision, itself a violent act, leads to more horrifying acts that are heaped on the Hivites and that end in the material enrichment of the brothers, who loot everything that survives their massacre. The message about conquering Canaan with blood, if necessary, cannot be overlooked.

Circumcision emphasizes exclusivity as well as separation. In the larger framework of Jewish history, circumcision evolved into the symbol of a divine association which appropriated for the Jews a strong sense of destiny. However, this sign, together with the strict dietary laws which were also "signs" of the covenant, led irrevocably to the Jews' isolation from other people. Jacob Katz's argument that major anti-Semitic eruptions were due to the voluntary decision on the part of the Jewish community to isolate itself from its neighbors is well taken.[15] Indeed, if one reads Jacob's reaction to the massacre of the Hivites (v. 30) with Katz's argument in mind, one detects in it that specific fear.

"Going Out"

Dinah is allowed only one simple, albeit crucial, act at the beginning of the chapter. But since her "going out" was related to foreign worship and sin, she was immediately silenced.[16] Everything that takes place in the tale subsequent to her "outing" is reported as done to her either by the Hivites or by her own family: first she is raped; then she is courted by her rapist, who attempts to communicate with her but ultimately negotiates with her father and brothers; further, she is snatched out of the house of her rapist by her brothers, who perform cruel acts of vengeance on her behalf. From a literary point of view, her absence is even more profound than her presence.[17] Additionally, the narrators seemed deliberately to have confused the personal moral issues in order to promote a national morality based on a political agenda promoted by a group of people who underwent a painful exilic experience.[18] Dinah was thrust onto a stage associated with forbidden religious rituals; her relationship with the Hivites was taboo for postexilic Jews, who painstakingly asserted that Israelites should marry their own kind and stay within the limits of the divine covenant which excluded all those who were "uncircumcised." Hence, the midrash on Dinah and the redacted version of the story are consolidated, and the audience is allowed a glimpse into the environment, mind, and political beliefs of those who shaped the story as it is told in Genesis.

The redactive agenda included a strong nationalistic prescription and instilled pride within the males of the community for accepting a spot in the cosmos created and governed by the mighty Yahweh. In fact, everyone who accepted Yahweh finally found a definite role to fill, including women. But the function of women turned out to be limited and heavily dependent on the males. It was the strong sense of destiny related to the covenant, coupled with nationalistic pride—belonging to the "chosen" nation who settled in and "returned" to the promised land—which, paradoxically, was disastrous for Hebrew women. Indeed, women were recognized as having the power to breed and perpetuate the race, but they were also perceived to be in need of watching over because of their proclivity to worship foreign gods and goddesses as well as because of their sexual nature. In a nationalistic context, women are called upon to perform functions that are basically biological. Furthermore, if portions of the nationalistic ambition are tied to land conquest, women are particularly limited because they are called upon to "supply" the nation with the necessary human "material" that would then undertake the role of warriors and conquerers. At all times, though, women were the weak link in the human chain and needed to be protected from the dangerous world outside the house of their fathers and brothers. Dinah was the consummate example of a woman who, when no male was supervising, went out to find other gods and strove to mingle with other people. As a result, she was assaulted by a stranger. But the brothers came to the rescue and she was snatched out of the house of her "tormentor" and returned to theirs. There is no textual condemnation of the act of the brothers mainly because, as was argued above, the redactors were fully supportive of the complete separation of Hebrews from Canaanites.

In more ways than one, this is the story of Simeon and Levi, who show, through the redactors' prism, a community that embraced narrow nationalism and exclusion. In fact, the extreme violence that pervades the whole chapter, generated by a desire to stay separate, was sometimes viewed with unease even by Jews who in principle agreed with the overall ideology of the redactors.[19] But the very decision to include the tale within Genesis, thus canonizing it, is a tribute to those among the redactors who felt confident about the world view that they were promoting. As scores of commentators and political activists throughout the ages have proved, the message was not misunderstood.

Portents of Nationalism

Marriage and Stability

When Shechem undertakes the courtship ritual, he approaches Jacob and his sons with generous terms: "Impose on me much dowry and gifts and I shall give as you will say to me, and give me the girl for a wife" (v. 11). In Shechem's mind, the relationship with Dinah can have only one acceptable ending: marriage. Furthermore, when Shechem engages his beloved's family, he is still struck by his love for her and he wishes them to like him as much as he loves Dinah. His statement "I want you to look upon me favorably" (v. 11) sounds sincere and can be attributed to his feelings of love for Dinah.

But when Hamor and Shechem appeal to Jacob and the brothers, they link the question of marriage with land acquisition and settlement. However, while emphasizing the positive Hivites' approach, it is impossible to ignore some glaring stylistic problems, especially in the major statements made by the perceived antagonists, Shechem and his family. The murky expressions used by them and the stylistically difficult formulations, which are abundant in the Hivites' speech, point to the process of redaction. But the contents of the Hivites' speech, confusion and all, convey the notion that marriage and land procurement, among those who have power, go hand in hand. The Hivites' invitation to the Hebrews involved in the Dinah matter hints at the possibility that the heroine's adventure was economically and politically inspired. Their entreaty, which brings up the topic of land, allows the brothers to challenge their sister's plan of integration. Because the main patriarchal preoccupation of Genesis is with the issue of legitimacy and the rights of inheritance, the brothers decide that the land of the Hivites is too precious to fall into their sister's hands. They, therefore, devise a plan that is consistent with their behavior throughout and calls for manipulation and deception. Their balanced argument presents the two elements that were the most dangerous for the redactors, namely, intermarriage and assimilation: "And we shall give you our daughters . . . and we will sit with you and become one people" (v. 16). The deceitful expression of the brothers outlined the apprehensions of the redactors, who were leading the Jewish community in the direction of nationalism—which, they believed, was the best way to ensure the Jews' survival.

The Land

When Simeon and Levi make their requirement of the Hivites, they bring up the subject of land and advance the story in terms of that issue, which would absorb the other aspects as well. The text suggests from the very beginning that they plot to "deceive"

(v. 13) — namely, to exclude and to kill the Hivites. For the Hivites, circumcision becomes a social sign of familial acceptability and they are ready to undergo the procedure even though they know that it involves pain and mutilation.

The brothers' attack on the circumcised Hivites is an example of the Deuteronomistic strategy of acquiring the promised land by annihilation. It contrasts sharply with the Hivites' public declarations of peace and prosperity for both peoples, and it eliminates any plans on the part of the Hebrews to achieve stability in Canaan through marriage — or, assimilation — with the people of the land.

The road to nationalism was intricate. The institution of marriage and the establishment of the family as the nuclear unit within the community were only the first steps taken toward the inauguration of a tightly knit group of people affiliated by blood, language, and territory. Indeed, historians are hard pressed to recognize nationalism in a cultural environment which paid tribute to large empires and syncretistic views, but nationalism did slowly evolve as a unique doctrine which defined one group's loyalties.

For the Hebrews, from the beginning of their political articulations, nationalism unfolded in a dualistic view of the world whereby two large entities, one of which was good and the other evil, were competing for supremacy. Since the Hebrews' primary political experience was anchored in Canaan/Israel and since the prophets became their main spokesmen of correct and incorrect political action, Jewish nationalism emerged as an ideology with typical prophetic ingredients. The most significant of these was embracing, in addition to Yahweh's judgeship and covenant, an extreme idealistic view of society, which pinned its hopes for a better life on a messianic figure who would deliver the covenantal members from dire circumstances. Even today Jewish nationalistic aspirations are tied to prophetic, messianic doctrines.[20]

Covenantal Separation

In the Dinah narrative, familial issues became communal matters, which points to the Deuteronomistic redaction. The writers used symbols charged with tribal — ultimately, national — emotions that were firmly fixed in a patriarchal past. Circumcision was one of these effective symbols; it brought to mind the covenant that Yahweh "cut" with the patriarchs, thus emphasizing exclusivity as well as separation. Circumcision was a positive sign (choice by God) as well as a negative one (the chosen have to commit themselves to social isolation). In the larger framework of Israelite/Jewish history, it indeed evolved into the symbol of a divine association which appropriated for the Jews a strong sense of destiny and identity. The latter made room for the settling of Canaan/Israel while the former placed the group on the stage of metaphysical history. Any attempts to disrupt the process were looked down upon, while efforts to materialize the procedure of settlement and entrenchment in the land were highly encouraged.

It may be further reiterated that Jacob, who, as we have seen, was quite insensitive to Dinah's plight, makes the point at the end of the narrative that his sons' actions were a setback in his attempts at integration into the new country. But Jacob is not the first Hebrew who tried to blend peacefully into the Canaanite environment, representing a different approach to land acquisition. Abraham buys a significant plot of land for the burial of Sarah (23:3–20), emphasizing first his "strangeness" in the land and therefore his willingness to pay as high a price as necessary for stability and affiliation. Isaac too tries to expand his Canaanite base and does it with some degree of success by claiming rights to some water sources (26:22). Jacob, undoubtedly, continues in the tradition that was started by his great patriarchal ancestors, but the story of Dinah introduces a solution to the question of settling Canaan which is much more radical, much more violent, and much more alienating than any of the answers attempted before.

*   *   *

The national mythology of the Hebrews emphasized their nomadic origins on the one hand and their desire for land and stability on the other hand. Inclusion in Canaan was only one of the steps taken by the patriarchs to signal their movement away from nomadic values and in the direction of civilized and centralized stability. But this in itself was not enough; therefore, when the redactors reviewed the Genesis stories, they adjusted them to the new ideological components which they deemed important so as to account for national permanence and commitment, which were lacking in the Hebrews' more nomadic stage.

The most momentous ingredient, typical of the new settlement in Canaan, was the covenant that Yahweh "cut" with Abraham, which dictated the course of patriarchal life in Canaan. In fact, Abram[21] seems to leave his home in Mesopotamia because he receives a call from Yahweh, who instructs him to go to a new country where great things will happen to him and to his family. The change that occurs when the patriarch decides to "obey" the voice of God and when the environment changes is not only in the life of the patriarch but in the life of his whole family as well. Locale is thus converted into a chief culprit as well as a main principle in Hebraic memory and history. In time, the "land" issue evolves into a complex web of intellectual and emotional responses that followed the Hebrews wherever they went even after they lost Canaan/Israel to the Babylonians in the sixth century B.C.E. and to the Romans in 70 C.E.

NOTES

1. D. N. Freedman maintains that, if we were to follow the tradition established in the Song of the Sea (Exodus 15), we would find that the makeup of the group that fled Egypt was not as heterogeneous as described by the redactors; they are "an undefined mixture of the stateless people at the bottom of the Egyptian class and power structure, sharing little more than a language" (*Pottery, Poetry, and Prophecy: Studies in Early Hebrew Poetry* [Winona Lake, IN: Eisenbrauns, 1980] 146). The Hebrew text refers to them as *ʿēreb rab* and *ʾăsapsup* ("rabble") (see Exod 12:38 and Num 11:4). It is thus entirely possible that the whole Israelite experience, specifically that which was associated with the Mosaic revolution and Yahweh, was in its very essence a "strangers'" uprising.

2. We have already emphasized the idea that the Deuteronomistic point of view, in light of the experience in Babylonia and the diaspora, was different from an earlier biblical perception which was more generous toward outsiders. In fact, with the advent of new diaspora and exilic concepts, there was a much more pronounced attempt to emphasize Jewish nationalism and uniqueness. The national enemies of the Jews were identified more and more with the inhabitants of the land of Canaan, and there was a clear dislike for those who stood in the way of the new generation of Israelites that finally emerged from the desert sojourn.

3. The Second Isaiah is the clearest example; see 56:5–6, where the

house of God is referred to as a "house of prayer for all peoples."

4. See especially R. P. Carroll's arguments in *From Chaos to Covenant* (New York: Crossroad, 1981). Also, it is worthwhile to recall the very restrictive Jewish environment that was created by Mishnaic and Talmudic scholars who followed the negative attitudes toward strangers of some of the biblical writers.

5. This is implied by M. Sternberg in "Delicate Balance in the Story of the Rape of Dinah: Biblical Narrative and the Rhetoric of the Narrative Text" (Hebrew) *Ha-Sifrut* 4 (1973) 193–231.

6. "Judaism regards speech as an event which grasps beyond the existence of mankind and the world. . . . The Word appears here in its complete dynamic as 'that which happens'" (M. Buber, *Israel and the World* [New York: Schocken Books, 1963] 16).

7. The most eloquent articulation of this particular facet of Jewish philosophy is Martin Buber's classical *I and Thou* (trans. R. G. Smith; New York: Charles Scribner's Sons, 1958).

8. See P. Trible, "Depatriarchalizing in Biblical Interpretation," in *The Jewish Woman: New Perspectives,* ed. E. Koltun (New York: Schocken Books, 1976).

9. There are a few interpretations which point to deceitfulness in the character of the Hivites. These also claim that the Hivites misrepresented their discussions with the Israelites to their own people and that Shechem was "lusting" after Dinah rather than really "loving" her. See, Sternberg, "Delicate Balance"; and Zakovitch, "Assimilation in Biblical Narratives," 185–92.

10. The word *midrāš* derives from the root *drš*, which means "to search," "to examine," "to investigate." See *Encyclopedia Judaica* (Jerusalem: Keter, 1972) 11:1507–11; see also Ofra Meir, *The Darshanic Story in Genesis Rabba* (in Hebrew) (Tel Aviv: Hakibbutz Hameuchad, 1987). Meir summarizes the major scholarly contributions to the concept of midrash since the beginning of the century and provides her own perspective as well. Meir's main argument is fairly simple and focuses on the genre of midrash as a unique combination of short story and sermon. The main portion of her book is dedicated to *Genesis Rabbah,* which is a collection of rabbinic *midrāšîm* that appears relatively late in Jewish literature (end of the Second Commonwealth), although the midrashic phenomenon itself is rooted in the oral tradition and hence is found in ancient sources. When the Torah assumed its authority, it became the central text in the life of all Jews, who attempted to find within its chapters and verses not only the words of God as they were transmitted to and through the prophets in the past but, more important, how these words might affect them in the present. The midrash became the vehicle that transmitted the words of the past into a present context. See also G. G. Porton, "Defining Midrash," in *The Study of Ancient Judaism,* ed. J. Neusner (New York: Ktav, 1981) 1:55–94.

11. R. Bloch, "Midrash," in *Approaches to Ancient Judaism*, ed. W. S. Green (Missoula, MT: Scholars Press, 1978) 1:35.

12. *Midrash and Literature*, ed. G. H. Hartman and S. Budick (New Haven: Yale University Press, 1986) xiii.

13. As E. A. Speiser had already argued (*Genesis* [Anchor Bible 1; Garden City, NY: Doubleday, 1964]).

14. Jacob's reaction to his sons' misdeeds detracts from his moral stature because not only does he not say a word about Dinah's terrible predicament, but he is concerned with matters of expediency and social status. After the rape and the brothers' atrocious acts, Jacob is merely worried about his good name (v. 30). It is this kind of response that further dehumanized women and led to men's flimsy treatment of their fears and emotions.

15. Jacob Katz, *Exclusiveness and Tolerance* (New York: Behrman House, 1961). The author argues that in addition to the physical separation between Jews and Gentiles, the emphasis on dietary restrictions as well as the peculiar dress code led European Jews to a not-so-splendid isolationist existence.

16. See Nehama Aschkenasy, *Eve's Journey: Feminine Images in Hebraic Literary Tradition* (Philadelphia: University of Pennsylvania Press, 1986) 124–33.

17. This should be compared with Tamar, who is very present and whose voice is very strong when the violent act against her occurs. We sympathize with her and understand very well what she feels. Indeed, in the story of Amnon and Tamar, there are obvious villains and heroes; the latter are associated with those who stand by Tamar and who also take revenge on her behalf (2 Samuel 13).

18. Note how even the brothers' villainy is not viewed as total wickedness; note also Jacob's a-moral reaction (vv. 30–31).

19. Even though it is very difficult to argue conclusively that Jacob's criticism of Simeon and Levi (49:5–7) was associated with their handling of Shechem and his village (see Y. Zakovitch, "Assimilation in Biblical Narratives," in *Empirical Models for Biblical Criticism*, ed. J. H. Tigay [Philadelphia: University of Pennsylvania Press, 1985] 190) it is interesting to note that throughout the ages, that connection has been made; see Rashi's commentary on that section. Clearly, the attempts to link Jacob's deathbed displeasure with his two sons and their deeds in Genesis 34 demonstrate an ambivalence expressed by some Jews who do not always feel very comfortable with the kind of violence that is described in the chapter.

20. For further study of this particular aspect of Jewish history, see, e.g., Walter Lacquer, *A History of Zionism* (New York: Holt, Rinehart & Winston, 1972) 40–42; Shlomo Avineri, *The Making of Modern Zionism* (New York: Basic Books, 1981); and Gary V. Smith, *Zionism: The Dream and the Reality* (New York: Barnes & Noble, 1974).

21. The name change occurs in 17:4 as an indication of the radical difference before and after the appearance of Yahweh and his covenant.

CHAPTER

5

A PARABLE FOR OUR TIME

THERE WILL BE NO ATTEMPT made in this section to characterize historically some of the contemporary problems facing Israel
and its neighbors (e.g., the Palestinians in the wake of the *intifadah*,
the Palestinian uprising in the Israeli-occupied [or "liberated"] territories, the West Bank of the Jordan River and the Gaza Strip).
However, the story of Dinah and her "stranger" can be appropriately
transformed into a parable for our time. The two characters, Dinah
and Shechem, can be viewed as victims of a rigid system that denied
them land, prosperity, and personal happiness. The method to be
used here to evaluate the meaning of the parable will be comparative, midrashic, and intertextual. Indeed, this section aims at
evaluating certain trends in Genesis that have a direct bearing on
ongoing events in the Middle East. Accordingly, we will approach
Genesis from the perspective of current events in Israel so as to
establish a contemporary midrashic parable that, in its turn, will
inform and illuminate crucial issues in Genesis. We will first focus
on women's silence in Genesis. Second, the story of Dinah will be
considered as a model of (1) tribal/national strife for territory,
(2) personal love and commitment, and (3) the inability of the
redactors of the text to accept women's active involvement in matters
of the heart or in matters of politics. Contemporary questions will
be taken into account in the third phase of this analysis.

The issue of silence in its various manifestations brings up the
"silent" ramifications of the exclusive nature of Yahweh, the concept
of the covenant and its connection to women's silence, and the link
between Yahweh's exclusivity, his covenant and circumcision, and
women's silence. All of these components converge in the story of
Dinah, the center of which is her silence. Even though Genesis 34
leads us to believe that the tale is about a woman, it is really about

two notoriously prominent Hebrew brothers (and/or tribes), Simeon and Levi. They are the main speakers and manipulators of the drama that unfolds. Dinah remains silent, and, in the final appraisal of the tale, it is this silence that must be accounted for.

Hebraic Territorial Rights

There are three elements that make up the explosive issue of Hebraic territorial rights: (1) the ascendancy of Yahweh, (2) the concept of the covenant that he "cut" with the patriarchs (rather than the matriarchs) of the Hebrew tribe (and nation), and (3) the sign of the covenant, namely, circumcision, which focused even more sharply on the importance, if not supremacy, of the males of the tribe. All of these components have been discussed in previous sections; their inclusion here serves to underscore their impact and to relate them to existing tensions between men and women, and Jews and Arabs, particularly, Palestinian Arabs.

The Ascendancy of Yahweh

Yahweh's ascendancy was completed in Jewish history at the time of the Second Commonwealth (sixth century B.C.E.–70 C.E.) when the Babylonian Deuteronomists and redactors of the Hebrew biblical canon accomplished their reform (some claim, their composition)[1] of Hebraic religion and introduced radically new concepts into the Jews' conduct of daily affairs. In other words, the religious agenda of the Deuteronomists was really aimed at a social, political program, and with the closing of the canon (second century B.C.E.) there was an ominous fastening of the doors on certain segments of society. For example, foreigners emerged negatively, and women were perceived as "naturally" dangerous and therefore in need of special treatment. The stranger was defined as that part of society which practiced "strange" rituals affiliated with gods and goddesses, especially of the fertility kind. Since strangers did not accept the supremacy and exclusivity of Yahweh, they were pronounced corrupt and corrupting. One must account for a deep psychological aversion to all those who did not share Israelite worship; this developed even more profoundly after the destruction of the Second Jewish Commonwealth (70 C.E.) and maintained its intensity throughout Jewish history. The attitude of Jews to all *goyim* (non-Jews) prevails in some sections of the Jewish community even today.[2] When that aversion was expressed ideologically, it was tied to the question of land, and Jews were exhorted to sever all contacts with strangers because of the dangers of assimilation and imitation.

Women were similarly dangerous, because they had a tendency to worship "other" gods and goddesses and they had considerable influence because of their function as mothers, responsible for the perpetuation of the race. Since it was impossible to dissolve all contacts with women, the latter had to be "contained" in some other way: hence, the strong ideological portrayal of women as weak, irresponsible, and frivolous. We saw in the preceding chapter that in the story of Dinah one finds a synthesis of all these womanly weaknesses. Dinah proved her frailty by succumbing to Shechem's sweet talk and remaining in his house while the negotiations with her family were in progress. She was fundamentally irresponsible because she went out of her house to "see the daughters of the land," which implied an attempt to socialize with those that the covenant excluded. From the redactors' vantage point, Dinah's thoughtlessness was manifested in her whole demeanor: leaving her father's house, not consulting with the males, remaining unprotected, and possibly going to the temple of the goddess in order to meet strangers in a strange land.

In order to present Yahweh as the most awesome substitute for the goddess, it was essential to portray him as the mighty God who had capacities that were not comparable to those of the goddess. Although the Hebrew Bible does not engage in a polemic with pagan religions,[3] the message in the text about Yahweh's superiority is unmistakable.[4] The goddess was associated with fluid, natural images, and the Hebrews portrayed Yahweh as the ultimate God of nature—implying that those who do not worship him are in some way "unnatural," if not actually corrupt. The idea of nature itself manifesting the greatness of God is typically monotheistic[5] and gives rise to similar concepts associating Yahweh with the very world we all live in.

But monotheism is far more than just a belief that highlights the superiority of Yahweh in the realm of nature. Monotheism is "directly antithetical to both the nature worship of primitive paganism and the anthropomorphism of mature paganism. . . .

From the very beginning, the God of the Hebrews is completely separate and distinct from the forces of nature. . . . [He] is the one who understands and who decides how the universe will function." Indeed, "God is the creator of the universe." By comparison, "pagan gods are born into an existing universe whose boundaries have already been fixed." Above all, Yahweh "is entirely apart from the universe that He has created. . . . He is not the subject, but the author, of the laws which govern the universe. They are but expressions of His will."[6] The originator, the governor, and the author, were roles that presented Yahweh as an incredible force that could not be easily, if at all, grasped by anyone. Paradoxically, this awesome, immutable entity was stubbornly intent on initiating a dialogue with people.

Yahweh's most intriguing, if not the most profound, characteristic was his verbal capability and, even more, his ability to engage a certain tribe (which evolved into a nation) in a dialogue that ultimately led to the tribe's unique position in the universe. This attribute is the most significant for the development of Jewish nationalism and uniqueness. It is expressed dialogically, and its complexity and philosophical genius[7] are manifested most fundamentally in the covenant. But before further commenting on the covenant, Yahweh's speech and communicative skills should be examined from the point of view of women. In other words, to whom does Yahweh speak and why? Whom does he not address?

Hebraic Memory, Silence, and Women

Land, memory, history, and women's silence are inextricably linked. Land was at the center of the Hebrews' struggle for permanence and continuity from the very early stages of the Abrahamic myth. Likewise, a link with the land was established at the very early stages of the Moses myth when Yahweh instructed his first prophet to "deliver" the Israelites from their enslavement not only to the pharaoh but also to other "foreign" gods and goddesses.[8] Moreover, that liberation was associated with a new life in a new land, Canaan. The psalmist, in line with prophetic pronouncements as well as in a politically charged statement, took the promise of land a step closer to fanatical nationalism by exhorting the masses: "If I forget thee, O Jerusalem" (Ps 137:6–7). Indeed, that declaration eventually became a rallying cry for great numbers of oppressed and politically deprived Jews in their diasporas.

Memory, a complex concept firmly linked with orality and history, is applied to the divine and human realms. Invariably, God "remembers" his promises (specifically to the patriarchs, e.g., Gen 9:15; Lev 26:42, 45), whereas the people "do not remember" (Judg 8:34; Neh 9:17; Ps 106:7). Actually, the people "remember" negatively: for example, when they are in the desert, they "remember" the "pots of flesh" that they ate in Egypt (Num 11:5) and they are ready to "stone" Moses, who brought them out "to perish in the desert" (Exod 17:1-4). When Ezekiel invokes the people's memory, it is also in a negative framework: "Remember your bad ways" (36:31), he calls out. What ultimately emerges out of the web of memory and forgetfulness is a relational pattern whereby the merciful, all-powerful God endows his chosen people with a territory and a set of laws that they have to accept and be grateful for. The people's share of the covenantal burden is simple and straightforward; namely, they have to "remember" Yahweh and his great deeds. The main event deserving of memory and celebration is the exodus, which ultimately led the Israelites to freedom and a political establishment in Canaan/Israel. But the negative context of remembrance is firmly maintained by the text's harping on the people's wrong "cleaving" to foreign gods and goddesses, especially during their sojourn in the desert: "Remember, do not forget that you have angered Yahweh your God" (Deut 9:7). Moses reminds the people time and again that their actions were undeserving, and, to further underscore their thanklessness, he admonishes them to "remember" it all. Similarly, when they are within Canaan, Joshua maintains the same ideological posture and warns the people about "not remembering" the Canaanites and their gods (23:7).

The connection between "remembering" foreign worship and women is closely established by the prophets and their Deuteronomistic followers. The popularity of the various goddess cults, as well as the heavy emphasis on women and sexuality within these cults, suggests that women were the main participants in foreign worship. Possibly, the early links between Hebrew women and the functions of priestesses in Mesopotamian and Egyptian temples helped further to focus on women's "vulnerability" with regard to non-Yahwistic assemblies. "So you will remember and be ashamed and not be able to open your mouth again because of your disgrace" (Ezek 16:63).

While God (particularly, Yahweh) "remembers" the various promises that he makes to the Israelites, he is also characterized as "remembering" some of the women in the text. The framework and occasions of "remembering" women are typically patriarchal; namely, God responds to the women's concern about their inability to bear children. In Genesis, Elohim "remembers" Rachel (30:22) before she finally gives birth to Joseph, and in 1 Samuel (1:19), Yahweh "remembers" Hannah before she gives birth to Samuel. Both of these women are psychologically devastated by their apparent "sterility"; both of them are the beloved wives of the men of the household; both have another fertile woman to compete with (Leah and Peninah, respectively); both first appeal to a male authority figure before finally being "rewarded" with a pregnancy (Rachel cries to Jacob, and Hannah appeals to Eli as well as prays to God). "Remembering" Rachel and enabling her to give birth to Joseph is ultimately an extraordinary redemptive event in Hebraic history and mythology. Not only are Joseph's father and brothers saved from the drought that afflicts the region, but they all "go down" to Egypt in order to return triumphantly after four hundred years of slavery. Also, in Jeremiah's oracles of eschatology, Rachel functions as the archetypal mother of the nation, who mourns her children and thus forces the hand of Yahweh. It is only after Yahweh hears her that he is moved to start the process of redemption (31:14–15). "Remembering" Hannah is similarly significant because of Samuel's ultimate "messianic" mission with regard to Saul, the first king of the Hebrews, and, more important, David, who is also mythically associated with the final redemption.

The pattern of memory and history suggested thus far points to a process by which God is the main factor in human affairs. But, at the same time humans take matters of memory and history into their own hands by struggling to maintain and acquire power and meaning. This is particularly poignant in the case of the women who cannot do anything about their barrenness and therefore verbally appeal to the deity. Rachel's outcry is described as an irritant to her husband, who bluntly and impatiently tries to silence her ("Am I God's surrogate who prevents you from carrying a child?" Gen 30:2). In the story of Hannah's long and desperate appeals to God, she appears to Eli, the main priest and power broker, as "drunk" (1 Sam 1:13-14). Like Jacob in Genesis, Eli too attempts to silence Hannah, but she prevails.

Dinah is one of the few women in Genesis who is effectively silenced. Although there is no overt reason for that textual silence, there is a clear indication that it is related to the act that she undertook at the very beginning of her tale. Dinah is described as "going out" of her house "to see the daughters of the land." After that act is presumably completed, she is neither heard from nor seen anymore. Instead of Dinah, Simeon and Levi take over as the main actors in that minidrama. Dinah is not like the other outspoken women in the text: she is not married, nor is she described as barren. She is a sister who suffers at the hands of a stranger who is ready to marry her only after violating her. On the face of it, Dinah's story is reminiscent of the Tamar and Amnon story, but even in the latter incident Tamar is allowed to speak and rebuke her rapist. Ultimately, Tamar mourns her brother's violation of her and only after that remains silent for the rest of her life.

When the "crying" women utter their desires in an orderly, patriarchal manner—that is, when they address issues that the males perceive as appropriately female as well as relevant to the men—they are heard. But if they are like Dinah, who went beyond female issues and dared to assert herself in a quasi-political way (going to see the daughters of the land), they are silenced. Politics is the domain of men; it is not part of the world of the "tent," where women rightfully belong.

The Covenantal Promise:
Yahweh, the Hebrews, and the Others

The covenantal promise made to the patriarchs and, throughout Hebraic history, repeated to major leaders (e.g., Moses) and prophets, evolved into a concept of monumental proportions. Not only did it establish a link with the world of the deity; it also forged a commitment on the part of the people, who were identified as the people of the covenant, to pursue certain ethical as well as political goals.[9] The territorial promise contained in the covenant had to lead to a politically active posture on the part of those who were pledged to it, and the articulation of the promise induced the Hebrews into adopting political attitudes that were not always benevolent. For example, the Mosaic version of the covenant directed Canaanite annihilation (Deuteronomy 7; 9) while Joshua's variant of the same demanded a protracted and expensive war which at its best was environmentally costly and at its worst morally debasing.[10]

Yahweh as a God of war was a far cry from the gentle goddess associated with rivers, the moon, and the seasonal cycles. Yahweh's covenantal missive was also very different from the simple message of immortality contained in the fertility cults. With immortality linked to war and devastation, as it was articulated in Yahweh's covenant and as the conquest of Canaan required, the Hebrews signaled their approval of physical brutality for the achievement of what they considered to be a loftier end. In this context, the involvement of Simeon and Levi in the Dinah affair is consistent with the biblical approach to Canaanite annihilation at the behest of Yahweh.[11]

The covenant introduced into the Hebraic equation fierce elements which sometimes contradicted more noble beliefs. In addition, although the covenant laid out the ground for a superb philosophy of dialogue and understanding, it also furnished and encouraged questionable ideas about morality and political behavior which had a lasting impact on Hebrews, Jews, and Western civilization alike.

Rape and Circumcision: The Social and Political Aftermath

Dinah and Her Brothers: The Woman as Chattel

One of the "signs"[12] of the covenant, circumcision, is clearly associated with male values. In fact, this mark was historically so compelling that Jews became solidly allied with it. In its more auspicious moments, circumcision is an emblem of separation which calls for a sharp division between peoples as well as between men and women. It is thus no accident that the story of Dinah focuses on the ritual and political aftermaths of circumcision. The only attempt to link the slaughter with the rape occurs at the end of the story, when the brothers respond to their father's rebuke. Moreover, the response is expressed in the form of a rhetorical question: "Will our sister be treated like a whore?" This device underscores moral righteousness and defiance. The brothers claim, with some measure of success, that their brutal actions belong in a narrow, familial arena; they insist that what they did was normal and acceptable. In their perspective, the issue is trivialized and delegated to the realm of private, family concerns that may have only a very limited impact. Not only do they appeal to a shrill, chauvinistic concern for private possessions (their sister's virginity is her most valued asset), but they declare open season on anyone who dares to question their judgment.

By playing off one issue against the other and by maintaining the tension between the private and the public, the narrators ultimately succeed in elevating the rape of Dinah into the realm of tribal confrontation. By juxtaposing the family of Jacob, who is first introduced as innocently going about its business of tending to flocks, with the family of Shechem, the man who seizes an unprotected woman, they manage at least to sow some seeds of doubt about the purity of the Hivite's motivation. By shrouding Dinah's motivations, by linguistically implying that she did something wrong, by not allowing her to speak, the authors open the door for the brothers. By permitting Simeon and Levi to scheme and manipulate, openly and with no reservation, they cast doubts on the impropriety of their actions. Being secretive implies guilt whereas openness suggests confidence and moral rectitude. The brothers remain openly and defiantly, to the very end, Dinah's avengers. In key phases of their operation, Simeon and Levi return to the violated woman—taking her out of Shechem's house and justifying their actions to Jacob—to remind us of the main reason for their deeds. They are unmistakably identified as "Dinah's brothers," who presumably know their obligations when a member of their family is threatened. But the supposed privateness of the affair does not overshadow the ultimate concern of the redactors, who, true to their own ideology and purpose, blame the trouble of the brothers on a careless woman who aimlessly "went out."

Individual Morality and Communal Political Action

The story of Dinah undertakes to draw the line between an individual's moral behavior and his/her social, political commitment. Further, it proposes that there is a link between the two, a tie that points to the individual's position in the universe. Thus, when Dinah exposes herself in a nontraditional manner—that is, not in order to look for a man of her own tribe and family who will take her as his wife—she is immediately penalized. Her unconventional action cannot be tolerated because if other women would use her as their role model, the whole community would be led into error and delinquency.[13] Moreover, Dinah's inability to speak about anything might imply that she agreed with the brothers' conclusions and saw no need to express herself. At least on one level, the text implies that her silence should be associated with embarrassment. It is almost as if there is a "correct" way to rape a woman (e.g., Amnon) and an "incorrect" way. In the case of Tamar she reacts indignantly because she was concerned about the health of her brother, perhaps even considering a union with him for purposes of power continuity; moreover, Tamar is instructed by David to attend to her presumed "sick" brother. Therefore, when the rape occurs, she has the "right" to complain and protest, whereas Dinah, who was not given permission by anyone of significant power to "go" anywhere yet did undertake an "outing," was, of course, wrong from the very start. Hence she has no "right' to speak.

When the brothers exact their revenge, they annihilate the whole Hivite community, not just Shechem (the responsible individual) and his household. Their action is thus colored by an ideology— not, as they say, by a wish to avenge the rape of their sister. The cruelty and the number of people affected by the brothers' operation point to an explicit attempt to place the whole affair within an ideological configuration. The story is therefore not simply about the woman Dinah and her rapist (as the brothers have it) but about a fundamental ideological breach that had to be corrected. Public responsibility is thus carried to new extremes placing every individual on notice. The totality of the ideology corresponds to the totality of the response to aberrant deeds within and without the community under consideration. Dinah's action was wrong from within, and she is appropriately handled not only by eternal isolation (clearly a communal rebuke) but also by silence, a form of death. The Hivites, the community from without, are collectively punished by actual death. Thus the narrators imply that the action of one individual was not just an offense that devastated another individual, but a deed that had communal ramifications and therefore was treated as a communal misdeed. This particular way of thinking, typical of extreme nationalism, is still prevalent.

The violent story of "the daughter of Leah that she bore to Jacob"[14] ultimately delineates the position of the Hebrews vis-à-vis the Canaanites and other "peoples" settled in Canaan. Furthermore, it sharply demarcates the family of Jacob/Israel from the neighbors among whom they settled. For example, the Israelites are circumcised and consider circumcision to be essential to their cultural and spiritual survival. The story defines what is and what is not acceptable behavior for Hebrew women; Dinah's appearance outside of the family's house, without the consent and/or knowledge of the male members, is doomed to failure from the very start. But it is particularly aggravated because of her encounter with Shechem, who is a Hivite wishing to intermarry and thus possibly "taint" the purity and exclusivity of those who were "chosen" to follow the covenant "cut" by God with the great ancestors of the tribe.

But without doubt, the revenge that the brothers undertake on behalf of their sister, is the most awful facet of the account. The wholesale killing of the Hivites raised eyebrows from the very start,[15] focusing attention on two distinct elements in the story: the reaction of Dinah's family and Shechem's reaction. The reaction of Dinah's brothers and father is typical of males with a patriarchal orientation who regard women as their chattel; specifically, the woman's rape was viewed not as a horrible experience that cried for sympathy and comfort but as a violation of property rights that cried out for compensation by force. Moreover, Dinah's loss of virginity was deemed an economic injury for the whole family because a nonvirgin's "bargaining" position vis-à-vis eligible males was considerably lessened.[16] Indeed, we never hear of what ultimately happened to Dinah after she was snatched out of her rapist's home. Because of that destructively male-centered attitude to raped women, it is no accident that both the brothers and the father show her no compassion. When Jacob does register his ire, he emphasizes the political and economic ramifications of the acts of his two sons — not a word of empathy for Dinah.[17]

The second focal point has to do with Shechem's reaction to the rape. If one is to find male compassion in the story, one has to turn to Shechem, "the stranger," who after the rape falls in love with Dinah and realizes that he must "console the girl" before proceeding with official, ritualized courtship. Excluding all the other difficulties that this peculiar order of events suggests, it is fair to observe (as the text unambiguously does) that the only man sympathetic to Dinah is Shechem, the presumed villain of the piece. In fact, it can be easily argued that Shechem's attitude is not only the most humane but also the most credible: how else could he have expected to live with Dinah, whom he had raped, as his wife? Not only did he have to place her on some pedestal for his own recognition, but he had to treat her as a person of worth if she was to carry on his family—especially since he himself was held in high esteem by his compatriots and was the son of a *nāśî'*, "chieftain." In the most bizarre twist of all, Shechem emerges as the heroic "Romeo" who falls victim to the mythical/historical hostility of his beloved's family. If there was no rape in the original core story, then the whole narrative can be studied as a comment on the impact of a stern agenda that placed land and possessions above moral and humanistic values.

The struggle for territory and the adherence to a group's set of ethics do not always go hand in hand. There is an even greater paradox in a liberation effort which presupposes from the very start that some people will be denied their freedom because the struggle cannot accommodate everyone. In the Zionist struggle, for example, there was always an overt as well as a hidden assumption that if the Jews were to return to their biblical "homeland," then the population that inhabited Palestine would have to share the burden or even be sacrificed. As a result of this attitude, the Zionist myth of "an empty country to a homeless people" became popular. In many ways, this myth was the equivalent of the biblical myth of "Canaan, the corrupt country to the chosen people." In both of these pronouncements, there was an expression of territorialism which maintained that even though the Hebrews/Jews do not naturally belong in the territory, they morally should have access to it. In the case of Canaan, Yahweh stepped into the moral void created by the corrupt, goddess-worshiping Canaanites, whereas in the Zionist example the world community supported the efforts of those who claimed that they were the moral backbone of the West and that they ought to be rewarded for serving as scapegoats and martyrs of numerous immoral causes throughout the European experience.[18]

The dichotomy between nature and morality is at the heart of the debate between the values of the goddess and Yahweh; she had been perceived as the perfect representative of the world of nature, particularly in its emphasis on continuity and stability. Harshness and violence were the opposite of the goddess's ideals because they ran contrary to notions of immortality and constancy. Yahweh, as the classical prophets presented him to the world and as the redactors fully consented, was the God of justice and morality; as such he rewarded the deserving and punished the wicked. The most significant models of corruption and evil in the Hebrew Scriptures were the Canaanites and the Egyptians, both of which cultures were goddess-oriented. Thus, the God of the Hebrews prescribed severe punishment for the Egyptians (hardening the pharaoh's heart, which became a collective symbol of nonrepentance) because of their harsh treatment of the Hebrews (*way'annûm*, "they tortured them"; Gen 15:13b and Exod 1:12, among many references), and total annihilation for the Canaanites, who were beyond redemption. Curiously, both of these acts—hardening the heart of the pharaoh and destroying the Canaanites—had complex political ramifications. As the Hebrews perceived it, they started their national journey toward Canaan as soon as they left Egypt and as soon as the pharaoh "let them go." Canaan was conquered only after there were several goddess purges within the camp of the Israelites during their desert journey (e.g., Deut 4:3).

Territory: Israelis and Palestinians

In Genesis, on a personal plane, there are two distinct references to the verb *'nh* ("to torture"): one is to Sarah's torture of Hagar after the latter became pregnant with Ishmael,[19] and the other is Shechem's "torture" (rape?) of Dinah. Both of these "tortures" remind the audience of the mythical enmity between the Israelites and the Egyptians and Canaanites. Also, both of these incidents have mythical, long-term consequences: the enmity between Sarah and Hagar is translated into the competition for the right to be Abraham's legitimate heir, which is transformed into the struggle between Isaac and Ishmael or, ultimately, Jews and Arabs. Isaac's supremacy is finally territorial. Similarly, the Zionist triumph is expressed territorially. But before both of these struggles reach their conclusion, there are two clear "losers," namely, Ishmael and the Palestinians. It is particularly worthwhile to observe the attitude of contemporary Israel toward land, the people who inhabit it, and moral values.

From before the inception of the modern State of Israel, territorial and moral issues were at the heart of the Zionist endeavor. Land acquired a mystical quality in some of the most significant Zionist pronouncements, and working the land was a major Zionist issue from the very start. David Ben Gurion, who went on to become the State of Israel's first prime minister, finally felt that "Hebrew work" (*'ăbōdâ 'ibrît*) was at the heart of the national endeavor. Even though the work ethic that he promoted had some suspiciously racist overtones, the slogan he created contributed to fostering new links between people who were basically urban and divorced from the land and the soil itself. While the Jewish nationalist urge demanded land and possessions, the Jewish élan, nurtured by decades of diaspora spiritual glory and actual suffering, viewed it with suspicion. From a feminist perspective, too much emphasis on land as a source of life, fertility, and communion with the divine leads to the objectification of women, who become associated only with the fertility of the soil and who are then expected—indeed, required—by the males to function as childbearers and mothers who sustain the great nation. Ultimately, it was suffering, on an unprecedented scale, that led to the creation of the state. In 1948, after bloody confrontations with a host of Arab nations, the Israeli Jews secured for themselves a territory; the price was high but it was morally justified because of the particular point in time in which it was accomplished. But territory came back to haunt the Israelis time and again; indeed, it still does. In 1956 there was the crisis at Suez, which led to the conquest of the Sinai desert; in 1967, there was the Six-Day War; and in 1973, there was the Yom Kippur War. Each time, the issue of the land became more ominous, more divorced from morality and compassion, more a pragmatic, political concern. In 1956, the territory conquered was abandoned for the sake of security, external and internal. In the aftermath of 1967, after a long period of bickering and at the instigation of Anwar Sadat, the late Egyptian president, more land was relinquished, presumably for the sake of peace and happiness. But since then, territory has been bitterly disputed between the Israelis and the Palestinians. The echoes of the brothers avenging the "rape" of their sister thus reverberate over the ages. But who is the sister? In the parabolic discourse at our disposal, the brothers were the ones who exercised their will and dictated the terms and the final outcome of their plan of action; they designed and maneuvered and "spoke." Similarly, it is the Israelis who are in control of their political destiny and who use the language of history and memory to defend and explain their actions. The Hebrew sister, Dinah, who dared to defy the system established in Genesis, posed a sexual and political threat because she was ready to intermarry and integrate with the Hivites. She shared other rebellious characteristics that were found in women like Eve, who was the arch-rebel of the text. Similarly, the contemporary "doves," who are ready to "talk" to the Palestinians, remind one of Dinah, who, textually speaking, just went out "to see" the Canaanites. By no accident, those among the Israelis who are prepared to talk and to listen are predominantly women activists who even have parliamentary representation and who strive for the removal of fanatical, religious constraints that in turn affect women more men.[20] However, Dinah's fate is duplicated in those who wish to embrace her "going out," because they too are silenced.

Silence

Scores of social commentators and philosophers have already observed that the greatness of a society is measured in its attitude toward the powerless, the "strangers," and the disenfranchised. The story of Dinah is of the powerless Hivites, who lost their "power" in the most essential way when they subjected themselves to circumcision and a kind of emasculation that rendered them impotent, who in the perspective of Israelite history were the "strangers," not to be tolerated by the people of the covenant. Dinah was the disenfranchised woman, who in a very real sense was excluded from participating in the covenantal promises and who had to submit to male values and rules at all times, even when these called for arrogance and lack of compassion. This "daughter of Leah" may have fallen in love with a "prince," thus stepping on ideologically sensitive toes. She was very quickly crushed and muted.

Silence is a powerful tool within the Hebraic tradition because it stands out as one of the most dreadful things that can happen to an individual within the chosen community. Silence is the opposite of discourse and communication, and losing one's voice is indeed losing one's identity and sense of belonging. It is quite significant that Shechem has a clear voice in the episode; he is heard privately, when appealing to Dinah, and he is also heard publicly, when negotiating with the brothers for Dinah's hand. But Shechem is emphatically silenced by Simeon and Levi.

Dinah is denied a voice and a family and remains a marginal woman in the text; her status as the raped and desolate daughter of Leah is firmly entrenched in the tradition. She becomes the prototype of other Hebrew women who have followed her footsteps and tried to mature independently of males and more inclusive of other people.[21]

Hebron and Shechem:
The Locus of a Parable for Our Time

In an attempt to link the Dinah affair with previous events in the text, the narrators tell us that "Jacob came whole [in good health; unharmed] to the city of Shechem in the land of Canaan . . . and he bought the piece of land [field], where he erected his tent, from the sons of Hamor the father of Shechem, for a hundred qĕśîtâ; and he established there an altar which he called El, the God of Israel" (33:18-20). The exchange between Jacob and the sons of Hamor, which is not described elaborately, clearly echoes the very detailed bargaining by Abraham for a piece of land in Hebron earlier in the text (chap. 23).

Ironically, there are now two clear geographical centers that serve also as symbolic centers in the confrontation between the Israelis and the Palestinians in the occupied territories. Both Palestinians and Jews attempt to show their strong links with these sites in order to carve for themselves a place in the heritage and a firm hold on the territories. Since our intent is to focus on events that are related to the Dinah matter, we will not analyze in detail the meaning of Hebron in the development of modern Israeli politics. Suffice it to say that settling Hebron by Jews and with Jews, eliminating Palestinian claims to it, and pointing out its significance as a major historical center for Jews have been on the Israeli agenda from the moment the city was conquered in the '67 war. It should be remembered that in the Genesis account where Hebron was first mentioned and where Abraham was involved in buying some of the land from the sons of Heth, the real purpose of the purchase was for Sarah's burial.[22]

The first time that Hebron is mentioned in the text is related to Yahweh's promise to Abram to "give" him the whole of Canaan: "And Abram made a tent and he came and settled in Elonei Mamre which is in Hebron and he built there an altar to Yahweh" (13:18). Similarly, when the Jacob settlement is narrated, just before the Dinah story occurs, the same "altar building" takes place. The narrators wished to establish a connection with this particular city not only by associating it with two major patriarchs but, more important, by telling us of the building of the altar, which reminds the heroes that Yahweh (or the God of Israel) should be praised and that his promise and covenant are kept intact. Both the covenant and Canaan are also symbols of the break with the past—which might have been more significant for the matriarchs, in a negative sense as we have seen. The continual emphasis on settling in a city and erecting an altar to the God of the patriarchs (rather than the matriarchs) further suggests that settlement in Canaan is first and foremost patriarchal. Certainly, when Abram leaves his Mesopotamian origins, he acquires status in the text and that, in itself, is quite significant.[23] In that sense, the link with Hebron has enormous impact because it is one of the first places that the narrators mention in connection with the family's new arrival in the land. The issue of naming a city or a place is of crucial importance to the creation of a certain perception of power and how it is distributed. Naming a thing is establishing authority in relation to it, as the creation narrative in the first chapter of Genesis suggests—when the man names his woman, after the catastrophe in Eden, she in effect, becomes his subject.[24]

Significantly also, Shechem is one of the original cities referred to in the Abrahamic text (12:6). In fact, the narratives suggest that Shechem was the first place that Abram reached on his arrival in Canaan, and it was there that Yahweh first appeared to him to tell him about the land and the covenant: "And Yahweh appeared to Abram and he said, I will give this land to your seed; and he built an altar there to Yahweh who appeared to him" (12:8). In another vital text, Joshua gathers the Israelites in Shechem in order to recite their history and to remind them of the covenant with Yahweh; the climax of this narrative is the burial of Joseph in the same plot of land that was bought by his father Jacob from Hamor (chap. 24).[25] Then there is the whole complex development of the Samaritan "sect," whose center of worship and ideology was Shechem and its adjacent Mount Gerizim. Although it is very difficult to glean from the textual evidence in Genesis any real presence of sectarian activity, it is possible that Yahweh and his covenant were deliberately interjected in the midst of a community that was either more tolerant of other gods or attempted to prove, as the Samaritans did later on, that it was the original Yahwistic assembly and that therefore it had the one and only "truth" from and about Yahweh.[26]

The Settlers and Their "Zumud"

We have established thus far a plausible link between the two cities under consideration and Yahweh, the patriarchs, and the covenant. We have also seen that it was important for the Israelis to seize Hebron as the shrine where their great patriarchal (and matriarchal) ancestors were buried. In many ways, capturing Hebron was even more important than conquering the Western Wall in Jerusalem because of the tremendous mythical impact of the stories of the patriarchs on the new generation of Israelis. Thus, when the phenomenon of the "settlers," first associated with Gush Emunim (the loyalists' bloc), reached symbolic proportions (after Menachem Begin and his Likud party seized political power from the traditional Labor government in the wake of the elections of 1977), Hebron was one of the first cities where violent confrontations between Jews and Palestinians took place. Now that the dispute affecting the two peoples has reached a critical turning point (in the wake of the Palestinian *intifadah*), Shechem is slowly becoming even more important than Hebron. To elaborate on the parable for our time, we will focus on the attitude of the modern equivalents of Simeon and Levi (namely, the settlers) and attempt to view their actions in line with the biblical formula instituted in the Dinah narrative.

Settling the occupied territories became an official policy of the government of Israel soon after the '67 war. The settlers were fully supported by the Labor government, which was even considering official annexation but was pressured, by the Americans, not to do so. Those who ultimately became "settlers" saw themselves as the pioneers of the sixties and seventies, comparable to those of the beginning of the century, with one major difference: they officially embraced the religious ideology of the Deuteronomists coupled with the messianic fervor of the later prophets and apocalyptists. The Labor government, which has been stagnant since its stunning military victory in the Six-Day War, was enchanted with the settlers because it perceived them as idealists who reminded those in power of their own youth and ideals.[27] Economically too the so-called creeping annexation policy began to pay off. But after the crushing military defeat of 1973 — the Yom Kippur War — and the continual helplessness and corruption of the Laborites, Begin was voted into office in 1977. The policy of territorial annexation took on a life of its own and quickly evolved into a deliberate attempt on the part of ideologically motivated Jews to solve the Palestinian problem by eviction, harassment, and annihilation. As is typical of groups that are nationalistically oriented, the settlers claimed that they needed to have all the physical, geographical space possible in order effectively to work the land as well as to realize their religious beliefs, practices, and life-style. For them, the Zionist dream was the dream of redemption and messianism, and for the latter to occur, one had to work the land and redeem it from any taint or blemish. In accordance with their Deuteronomistic approach, they maintained that there is only one people who are the legitimate owners of the land. As Rabbi Isaac Ginzburg, the head of the main Yeshiva erected in Shechem, proudly asserted: "Eretz Israel [the land of Israel] belongs to one people only, that is, the people of Israel."[28] And how does one assure that "belonging"? "If a Jew gets up [rebels] out of real hurt and jealousy [connotes outrage] for the Shechina [the Divine presence], [or because of] jealousy for the honor of Israel, and does something [namely, violence], I appreciate it." It was the same "spirit of jealousy" (presumably because of what was done to their sister) that prompted the brothers to destroy the Hivites. But beyond the purely nationalistic motivations of the settlers, there is another element that must be accounted for and which was awkwardly articulated by Israel Lebowitz, a student at the above yeshiva:

> Identifying with Shechem is like identifying with something enigmatic. This city is somewhat Canaanite. Its landscape is massive and indeed, the nation of Israel was built as a result of its confrontation with Canaan. I cannot say that this was a trivial confrontation. Canaanism breathed (was defined by) the world (the material). I would say that it was swallowed into it. And I feel that we, as people,

should not give up these basic feelings, this immediate connection with nature. . . . I feel that we must free ourselves from our naïve attitude to nature, in order to reach the very roots of our body; not to surrender to them, but rather to live them. All of that connects in my mind with Shechem. Because Shechem is something very basic. Something which is pre-Jerusalemite. It is not like returning to a climax, Jerusalem is the climax; it is like returning to the beginning which we miss so much, to the real attitude to a material being. . . . I feel that the religious people never penetrated the world of the material and that the secular people forgot about it.[29]

The chief concern of Lebowitz is a distinctive attitude that he identifies with Shechem; he refers to it as "pre-Genesis," "pre-Jerusalem," "mystical," "Canaanite," "material," "natural" — all of which combine to denote primitive as opposed to civilized and real as opposed to contrived or intellectual. For Lebowitz, Shechem is a state of mind which arouses basic feelings. One such feeling is essentially original and powerful and in that sense is hard to articulate and define. It is a condition that was shared by all people before they were separated by a variety of ideologies and racial and/or religious differences, before intellectualism interfered with the basics of existence. Even though Lebowitz attempts to insert a certain derogatory value to the concept of Shechem, he actually expresses an appreciation for something which is more binding, earthy, real — perhaps of a female nature — which is totally lost to him and his compatriots. On the other hand, Shechem is perceived by Lebowitz as parallel to nature, which was a traditional subtheme in the Jews' attempts to verbalize their nationalistic feelings. Since, by and large, the Jewish European experience was urban and thus divorced from "nature," the question of working the land and restoring a lost value was, at one point, quite prominent in the Zionist quest. Rabbi Abraham Isaac Kook (1865–1935) was the main Zionist spokesman for a mystical ideology of land and redemption, which is echoed in the words of Lebowitz:

The claim of our flesh is great. We require a healthy body. We have greatly occupied ourselves with the soul and have forsaken the holiness of the body. We have neglected health and physical prowess, forgetting that our flesh is as sacred as our spirit. We have turned our backs on physical life, the development of our senses, and all that is involved in the tangible reality of the flesh, because we have fallen prey to lowly fears, and have lacked faith in the holiness of the Land. . . . man proves his faith in eternal life by planting.[30]

In a rather amazing assertion, Kook equates the power of the flesh, traditionally associated with women and their activities, with that of the spirit. He goes on to voice an opinion that regards the land as sacred and emphasizes "planting" in the context of immortality. In that sense, Kook compares the power of the earth with ideals and concepts promoted by worshipers of the earth goddess. In his own crude way and without referring his remarks to Kook, Lebowitz pronounces the same idea, which motivates him to go into the village of Shechem, claim it as his own, and dispose of its inhabitants. Thus, the danger of an ideology which fosters the holiness of the land is apparent: the emphasis shifts very quickly from people to the land itself. In other words, in order to justify the settlers' attitude to the Palestinians, they tend to ignore the people who happen to be on a tract of land and center their interest on the land, thus rendering the people worthless. Shechem, not the Shechemites, is filled with values and aspirations; the village/city has significance, not the people who might have inhabited it in the past or in the present. In Lebowitz's terms, "Canaanism," not Canaanites, is appealing and should be incorporated into Israeli life. Indeed, this is a process of objectification and estrangement which makes it possible for the settlers to proceed with their violence against the "stranger" population. This was also the attitude of the Deuteronomists and the redactors of the biblical text. Their mythology was geared toward hallowing the land in whose center even Yahweh chose an abode. The Israeli journalist Yoram Binur, who for six months posed as an Arab in Israel, made the point that the worst experience he had during that time was not being beaten or ridiculed or harshly treated, but being totally ignored. In one of the most dehumanizing episodes experienced by Binur, he describes two Israeli Jews, a man and a woman, who entered the kitchen where Binur was employed and proceeded to make love as if he did not exist, let alone have any useful function in the place.[31]

The condition of nonexistence, or "invisibility," as Ralph Ellison might have it, is very close to the state of silence, which is one of the strongest weapons used by the settlers in their current struggle against the Palestinians. Silence is clearly manifested in the settlers' treatment of "the enemy" and more specifically in the language that they use in order to describe that foe. The demonization process has been so complete that there is some concern among historians — even journalists — and some progressive politicians that the key to the solution to the Arab–Israeli conflict has already been thrown into the ocean and that the two communities directly involved will be locked in battle until the bitter end. In fact, there are disturbing psychological and sociological reports from the Palestinian camp which claim that the social and traditional order has been shattered to such a degree that any healing will be difficult, if not impossible, to undertake. Moreover, because children are in the forefront of the struggle against the Israelis and because their parents are less active in resisting the occupiers, the breakdown of parental authority is of enormous consequence. The rules that are set up to fill the authority gap are much more intangible, but they tend to be more rigid, more ideological, and strongly linked to a fanatical kind of fundamentalism which further contributes to the hardening of political positions and to the ineffectuality of compromises.

In the meantime, the settlers perform acts of violence against individuals who are viewed as fodder for their guns and slings. When sixteen-year-old Evetsam Buzia was shot in the head and heart while standing at the window of her home at Kaffel Harath, the settlers' response was that their own Ilana Raphael of Kiryat Arba was injured by a rock thrown on a car. The structure of the ancient parable is thus maintained perfectly, namely, a woman is injured (Dinah was raped) and revenge must be taken; it must be as violent, as prompt, and as unjust as can be because only if it is extreme can it accomplish the purpose which provides the avenger(s) with false power and which characterizes him (them) as the master who can arbitrarily undertake any action that will wreak havoc among the weak strangers.

The underlying association between the woman and the land which objectifies the woman provides an ideological excuse for the violent perpetrator. The "stranger" becomes a stranger (rapist) to the woman as well as to the land. He not only performs evil acts on women; he also does not belong on the land which he claims is his. When Yitzhak Shamir publicly objected to the establishment of a Palestinian state on the West Bank and Gaza, he used pointed words which were linked with the above ideology and mentality: ". . . they

[Palestinians] are brutal, wild, alien invaders in the Land of Israel that belongs to the people of Israel, and only to them." Thus, when the avengers (the brothers and the settlers) take on the outsiders/demons/evildoers they too wave the flag of rightful owners whose function it is to "redeem" the defiled woman/land. The ominous metaphors used by the classical prophets to describe the function of women in the cult and in the land prior to its destruction, came back to haunt the Deuteronomists in the past as they do Israelis in the present. It is therefore no accident that the most horrifying violent acts that occur today in the occupied territories involve vengeance on behalf of women and/or girls who seem to be in danger.

But, even more significant, violence is now perpetrated by those settlers who practice a relatively new policy which expresses their almost intimate relationship with the land, "Zumud," namely, staking out a claim on the land by sheer persistence. The term Zumud was coined by the Baghdad conference in 1978 to characterize the condition of the Palestinian refugees in the various camps.[32] In the 1980s, the settlers, who in addition to building new settlements and dispossessing the Palestinians, also venture out on tours and walks across the occupied territories, practicing their own kind of "Zumud." These "innocent" activities enable them to be present constantly where they are least wanted; it also permits them to provoke confrontations and fabricate situations which demand immediate violent action. In one of the more sardonic occurrences of this kind, Tirzah Porat, a teenager who was on her way "to tour the land" (with other settlers),[33] was accidentally shot by her own protectors, who then proceeded to shoot Palestinians indiscriminately. The most ironic part of this incident was that local Palestinian women attempted to shield the Jewish girl from the fate that finally befell her.

Zumud, while clearly attempting to respond to a problem related to the Palestinian situation, has a corollary in the Israeli experience that is relevant to the question of women and strangers and which also addresses the issue of "touring the land." From a very early time, the Israeli educational system incorporated within it the concept of "knowing the land" (yĕdî'at hā'āreṣ). It is related to an intellectual as well as a geographical/physical knowledge of the Israeli terrain. A whole generation of Israeli-born children (Sabras) grew up with a deep appreciation for the natural beauty of their country. In a way, they grew up to know physically the various nooks and crannies of the land, thus establishing a strong bond with the landscape itself. Touring the country was a *sine qua non* of every child's school curriculum, and at least once a year students would be launched on various trips for extended periods of time. A whole culture and concomitant rituals were formed, and new concepts were introduced in order to accommodate this important activity. For example, a tour that was referred to as "from shore to shore" included an extensive excursion of the beaches of the Mediterranean Sea as well as the Jordan River, which implies that these are the "natural" west and east borders of the land. Other popular routes included the various mountains associated with biblical incidents and the ominous desert region, where one had to be well-equipped with water. The knowledge that students acquired on these trips was of immense value not only educationally but socially and psychologically as well.

But we have seen that "knowledge" is a highly charged word in the vocabulary of the Hebrews. Although the Tree of Knowledge contained various concepts, it was also a tree that unraveled some of the secrets of sexuality. Certainly, when the man "knew" his woman and she conceived, that knowledge was purely sexual. Decoding the concept "knowledge of the land" leads us into the realm of sexual images coupled with conquest and violence, because the ultimate aim of "knowing" the land was indeed "clinging" (zumud) to it; in fact, the more you "knew" it, the better you mastered it, the more of a claim you had on it. In this context, the metaphor is oppressive and conjures up ideas about the position of women as well as strangers in the land, the latter of whom have to be exiled ultimately because they cannot be privy to the same "knowledge." The current phenomenon thus corresponds to the past and gives us additional insight into the actions of the patriarchs and brothers in Genesis. By annihilating the Hivites, by eradicating their village, and, even more so, by erecting new altars to new gods, by naming new names, the process of the Israeli zumud reaches its climax, as it did in the tale of Dinah.[34]

* * *

The dark aspects of monotheistic faith are present in all three monotheistic religions. Holy wars have been fought from the beginnings of monotheism, and many innocent people have lost their lives because of the strict demands presumably put forth by the deity. Catholics and Protestants are still at each other's throats in Ireland; Moslems and Christians fight it out in Lebanon, and there are various "Ayatollahs" (including Rabbi Meir Kahane) trying to forge their mark on the world. "Strangers" do not fare well in those communities, and neither do women, as I have tried to demonstrate. But part of the unsung message of the story of Dinah is that it is possible — at least externally — to alleviate the lot of the powerless and the excluded by first recognizing each other's humanity and by deemphasizing exclusion and separation.

We have seen that in a number of crucial texts the Hebraic tradition is very eloquent about the fate of "orphans, widows, and strangers." It is particularly sensitive to the destiny of have-nots, and time and again it attempts to identify itself with those who are unfortunate. Accounting for "the other" is indeed a Jewish tenet, and it is "the fact that one person sets another at a distance and makes him or her into an independent other that enables the person to enter into relation with others. Through this 'interhuman' relation, people confirm one another, becoming a self with the other. Mutual confirmation is essential to becoming a self."[35] Dinah's "going out" fits the taxonomy of inclusion and mutuality, and in that perspective her ideal, unredacted story should be the parable for our time.

NOTES

1. For a literary-historical analysis of the Deuteronomists and their impact on the whole of the tradition, see R. Polzin, *Moses and the Deuteronomist* (New York: Seabury, 1980).

2. See some of the more notorious parts of Philip Roth's *Portnoy's Complaint* (New York: Bantam, 1970), where the protagonist points to his family's intolerance of *goyim*. Roth deliberately emphasizes food and eating habits, which make Jews different and which further enrage his protagonist.

3. See Yehezkel Kaufman, *The Religion of Israel*, trans. M. Greenberg (Chicago: University of Chicago Press, 1960).

4. In numerous texts, if not overtly then certainly indirectly, Yahweh is contrasted with ineffectual deities; the most classical example is Elijah's

sarcastic appeal to local gods, who seem to be inoperative at a time of very great need (1 Kgs 18:27–30).

5. See, e.g., Psalms 19:1–7; 136.

6. M. Carella and I. Sheres, "Hebraic Monotheism: The Evolving Belief, the Enduring Attitude," *Judaism* 37 (1988) 237.

7. Martin Buber's dictum of I-Thou is, in its very essence, based on the covenant between God and man. For a historical, philosophical analysis of Buber's position, see *The Prophetic Faith* (New York: Collier Books, 1977).

8. There are various stories (midrashim) about Abraham's commitment to Yahweh which emphasize his early "purge" of other gods that were a part of his and his ancestors' household.

9. In the book of Deuteronomy there is an attempt to present the issue of the conquest of Canaan within both an ethical and a politically pragmatic framework. The Deuteronomists clearly maintain that there is a dichotomy between the ethical ideal which upholds life's holiness and which provides for the administration of justice (particularly where weaker segments of the population are concerned) and the more pragmatic concept that if people are to acquire territory they will have to resort to violent means that at times will be directly opposed to the theory of justice. See 7:1–11, where the emphasis is on the destruction of the Canaanites because of the covenantal promise as well as because of the "specialness and holiness" (*s̆ĕgullâ* and *qĕdûšâ*) of the Israelites; also 9:3–6, where the emphasis is on the evil nature and deeds of the peoples of Canaan and where the Hebrew nation is characterized as "stubborn and undeserving."

10. There are pertinent examples in Joshua 5; 6.

11. The contemporary Israeli counterpart to the idea of covenantal annihilation is crudely, but realistically, articulated by Rabbi Meir Kahane in *Our Challenge: The Chosen Land* (Radnor, PA: Chilton Book Company, 1974). Appropriately, the author opens his arguments with two separate quotations from Deuteronomy (7:6 and 11:24–25). One should not underestimate the appeal, especially now that the *intifadah* is taking a severe psychological and economic toll, of Kahane's extreme solutions to the Arab–Israeli conflict. While it is still not popular openly to advocate annihilation, Israelis view favorably the notion of Palestinian resettlement (someplace outside of Israel/Palestine) and banishment (especially of threatening figures who are viewed as "potential leaders and troublemakers").

12. There are three signs of the covenant, circumcision, the Sabbath (Exod 31:17), and the dietary laws (Leviticus 11; Deuteronomy 14).

13. All individuals must be held accountable for their actions not only because of the emphasis on individual responsibility but also because of the communal ramifications of individual action. Achan's betrayal in Joshua 7 is the most glaring example.

14. The language that is used in the text reveals the attitude of the writers to the presumed heroine, who is neither heard from nor reacts to

any of the things that take place in the narrative. There is subtle contempt for Dinah, who is viewed throughout the ages (Rashi's commentary is the most representative) as a woman who "went out" with sex on her mind (like her mother Leah before her in Gen 30:16). Because of that she was perceived as actually inviting a rape.

15. See the various interpretations of the story, some of which present outright disgust with the deeds of the brothers. Y. Zakovitch is one of the more recent analyses ("Assimilation in Biblical Narratives," in *Empirical Models for Biblical Criticism*, ed. J. H. Tigay [Philadelphia: University of Pennsylvania Press, 1985] 185–92); practical indignation as expressed by Jacob is, ironically, the first of the negative reactions.

16. Among the requirements for marriage in Genesis, virginity was a *sine qua non*.

17. It is also quite unlikely that on his death-bed when Jacob articulated his disenchantment with Simeon and Levi, he was thinking about the Shechem affair. See Zakovitch, "Assimilation in Biblical Narratives," 190.

18. There are myriad examples of real and perceived anti-Semitic incidents which Jews finally used in order to articulate the cause of Zionism. By no coincidence, the Zionists reaped the results of their efforts only after the Second World War. Also by no coincidence, the first big push toward the creation of a politically viable Zionist party (with Theodore Herzl as its founder) came on the heels of the Dreyfus affair in France at the end of the nineteenth century.

19. See particularly the very sensitive analysis of P. Trible (*Texts of Terror* [Philadelphia: Fortress, 1984]).

20. Shulamit Aloni has been advocating the rights of women within the context of the party that she founded called the Citizens Party. She is viewed with disdain (sometimes referred to as traitor) and her political survival is at best marginal.

21. There are a few women in Israel today who try to organize small communities of rapprochement with the Arabs; one that readily comes to mind is "Gesher," which (as its name implies) attempts to create a bridge between the two societies. Its base is in Haifa, and its members engage in mutual visitations where both parties, Jews and Arabs, learn firsthand about each other's daily routines. Not by accident, women make up the majority of the members of Gesher. Similarly, the more activist and intellectually inclined group, Women in Black, holds weekly vigils in Haifa calling for an end to the occupation of the West Bank and Gaza. Then there are those who actively attempt to bridge the political gap by engaging in a dialogue with the P.L.O. (Palestine Liberation Organization). The case of Michal Hadas, a journalist, is of particular interest because she is now under indictment, perceived as a traitor and silenced in a jail. There are also international women's conferences which focus on Israeli–Palestinian

discourse featuring women from both camps; the last important conference was in Brussels in June 1989.

22. The purchase is narrated at a crucial point in the development of the Abrahamic saga, namely, right after the miraculous episode involving the sacrifice of Isaac (Akedah). Traditional and classical commentators attempted to show obvious links between the death of the matriarch and Isaac's predicament. Also, there are clear connections between Isaac's survival as the one and only heir to the covenant and Ishmael's rejection of the same. Ironically, Moslems claim that it was not Isaac who was almost sacrificed on Mount Moriah; rather, it was Ishmael.

23. In the encounter with pharaoh, for example (12:10–17), Sarah's position is quite prominent, even though the text tries to cover it up by focusing primarily on her feminine, sexual attraction.

24. See P. Trible, *God and the Rhetoric of Sexuality* (Philadelphia: Fortress Press, 1985); she makes the point that the man dominates and reduces the woman "to the status of an animal by calling her a name" (p. 133).

25. Robert G. Boling and G. Ernest Wright summarize current scholarship about the connection between Joshua and the Deuteronomists (*Joshua* [Anchor Bible 6; Garden City, NY: Doubleday, 1982] esp. 66–72). Regardless of whether the whole of the text is Deuteronomistic or not, there is no doubt about the ideology expressed in the text, which is similar to that of Deuteronomy and has been used throughout the ages to signal Canaanite destruction and Israelite election.

26. For a preliminary view of the Samaritans and their ideological origins, see James D. Purvis, *The Samaritan Pentateuch and the Origin of the Samaritan Sect* (Cambridge, MA: Harvard University Press, 1968).

27. The early concept of "conquering the wilderness," which was used by the Zionist settlers at the beginning of the twentieth century, became a political and economic hallmark. It spilled over into the realm of ideology and psychology claiming that the Arabs did nothing with the land—in fact, they "wasted" it—and therefore did not deserve it. The view of Zionism as a progressive, positive, scientifically oriented force was compared with the Arabs' perceived backwardness, primitivism, and laziness. All of that is not very different from the traditional colonialists' view of natives in an occupied territory.

28. (Hebrew) *Ha'aretz* (June 2, 1989).

29. Nadav Shragai, "The battle over the tomb", *Ha'aretz* (June 2, 1989).

30. *The Zionist Idea*, ed. A. Hertzberg (New York: Meridian, 1960) 431.

31. Yoram Binur, *My Enemy, My Self* (Garden City, NY: Doubleday, 1989).

32. See David Grossman, *Yellow Wind* (Hebrew) (Tel Aviv: Hakkibutz Hameuchad, 1987). There is a certain irony in the use of an Arabic word to describe an Israeli situation, as is also discussed in Grossman's book.

33. Reminiscent of the activities of the spies sent out by the Israelites before their entry into Canaan (Deuteronomy 1). Interestingly enough, the "bad report" that they submitted to the grumbling community instigated the severe punishment of wandering in the desert for forty years.

34. Meron Benvenisti, *The Sling and the Club* (Hebrew) (Jerusalem: Keter, 1988).

35. Maurice Friedman, "Dialogue, Confirmation, and the Image of the Human," *Journal of Humanistic Psychology* 28 (1988) 123.

THE OTHER STORY:
THE UNREDACTED VERSION

THERE IS NO QUESTION about Dinah's importance in the text. Not only is she the daughter of Leah, who was a fertile matriarch and the mother of six males all of whom were the patriarchs of notable Hebrew tribes, but she is actually named, contrary to other unnamed women, some of whom by their outright relation to the males were quite important (e.g., Noah's wife, Judah's wife, etc.). Even more directly, Dinah's importance is accentuated in the text in comparison with the other "daughters of Jacob" (37:35) none of whom is explicitly mentioned except in the above very brief statement, the subject of which is the patriarch's mourning over the presumed death of his beloved son, Joseph.[1] In fact, Dinah's birth (30:21), her first mention in Genesis, precedes the birth of Joseph, and she is last cited in the book, just before the Jacob family is reunited in Egypt with the patriarch's long lost beloved son (46:15). Hence, the narrative sequence of Dinah's affair (chap. 34) falls between the birth of Joseph and the description of his various activities. And Joseph is not just the favorite son of the family's patriarch, but he evolves into a powerful Egyptian lord.

The story opens with Dinah, whose name is significant (even though there is no direct name description associated with her, as there is with all the male descendants), because it places her within a deeply religious context: *dîn* in Hebrew refers to religious law closely affiliated with justice, the source of which is divine.[2] She is also identified as "the daughter of Leah," that is, her mother's daughter first and foremost. In a patriarchal text where genealogies are male related and the patrilineal line is safeguarded by the father, it is significant that Dinah's relation to Leah seems to be more important than her relation to Jacob. This particular aspect of the story is worth highlighting because even when Jacob finally does react to the events that occur in the chapter, he is not terribly upset about what actually happened to his daughter but rather about the possible social and political ramifications of the brothers' deeds. The text thus seems to draw a line between the mother's function (and maybe invested power) and the father, who is always attached to his sons (preferably, the firstborn) rather than his daughters.

However, it is entirely possible that Jacob's reaction, which was directed mainly toward the violence that Simeon and Levi were closely connected with, fits a more original version of the story, where there was no rape. Moreover, since the dreadful events of the chapter report the two brothers' destruction of a whole village, it is conceivable that another, more original narrative described events that may have occurred in the vicinity of Shechem and had to do with a bloody confrontation between the two tribes of Simeon and Levi and the tribe of the "Hivites" who were settled in Shechem. Since the tribe of Simeon was ultimately absorbed by the tribe of Judah and since Levi had "no inheritance" (e.g., Josh 13:14, 33), the narrated events inform us of how these two tribes might have lost their inheritance. (We will see more about "the Hivites" and the two Israelite tribes further on.)

As for Jacob in relation to Dinah, when the text first mentions him ("that she bore to Jacob"), it alludes to another incident in 30:21, where the general background for Dinah's birth is narrated. The text employs the verb "to go out" in connection with Leah, who is at that time seeking to sleep with Jacob in one of the many instances of sisterly competition for sexual favors. When Leah "goes out" to sleep with Jacob, she gives birth to a fifth and a sixth son (Issachar and Zebulun). Her last born, mentioned only casually, is a daughter, Dinah. Bearing in mind the meaning of Dinah's name, is it possible that her birth bears witness to Leah's power and "just" (legal) stature in the text? Is there personal "justice" for Leah, who by giving birth to a daughter, who presumably will be closer to her mother (compared with the sons who traditionally adhere to the father), is thus assuring her individual legacy? In another vein, the implied "justice" in Dinah's name illuminates the injustice meted out to her mother throughout her married life with Jacob. He does not want her, nor does he love her. Leah seems to be forced on Jacob because of her father's perception that nobody wanted to marry her. A daughter who seems sometimes to repeat very crucial events in the life of her mother could "correct" that injustice and perform actions denied to her mother. "Going out" to meet a daughter's future husband seems to be a fundamental activity undertaken by the major matriarchs in the text while they are still in their father's homes (e.g., in 24:15 Rebekah "goes out" to water the flocks of her father and meets Eliezer, Abraham's house manager, who is looking for a bride for Isaac; and in 29:6, Rachel "came out" to water her father's flocks and met Jacob, who fell in love with her at first sight; see the discussion in chap. 3). Leah did not perform this particular ritual, whereas Dinah seems to do precisely that at the very beginning of the narrative. Throughout Genesis, although there is a clear preference for the patrilineal arrangement, it is the younger son who usually receives the father's blessing and inherits the divine covenant.[3] The very presence of a matrilineal system bears witness to its existence either at the time the text was redacted or at an earlier stage when the text was closer to its oral roots, or both. It should be noted that within the Hebraic tradition (specifically in the Pentateuch), there are a few examples of women who do have access to important legacies and acquire possessions similar to those of men.[4] As for Dinah, even though she was Leah's last born, there is no textual indication that she had access to an inheritance.[5]

Immediately after the birth of Dinah, Rachel gives birth to her first son, Joseph, whom she proclaims to be the symbol of "the removal ('āsap) of her shame" (30:23) as well as a sign of "more to come (yôsēp)" (30:24). The birth of Dinah, which has (at the very least) sentimental value for Leah, is textually balanced by the birth of Joseph, who is enormously prominent in the text and steadily acquires an independent voice—unlike Dinah, whose value slowly erodes and whose voice is muted. Another curiosity related to Joseph (and Dinah) is the link with Shechem: Joseph is ultimately buried in Shechem.

One cannot overlook the strategic position of the whole of the family of Jacob, who are described as just returning from their home in Aram/Haran, where Jacob served Laban for more than twenty years. In fact, all of the Hebraic sagas, starting with Abraham, are closely related to Haran. Genesis firmly identifies Abraham's origins with Haran (11:31 and 12:4), and the other patriarchs are connected to it as well. By no coincidence, that connection is primarily through the women: Isaac takes Rebekah, who is from Haran, as his wife; and Jacob "flees" to his family in Haran from the wrath of Esau. All of Jacob's children (with the exception of Benjamin) are said to have been born in Haran, including Dinah. At the very least, the Haran tradition in the primary history of the Israelites is consistent and sound.

Since a named woman in any text warrants study and investigation, Dinah's name and implied history are even more important because she is the only named daughter of Leah. The survival of her name indicates that there might have been an elaborate story, maybe a whole tradition, associated with her. The Masoretic Text, which is the product of editing and redacting, relates that story in chap. 34, deemphasizing the woman and highly profiling the brothers (male tribes). However, because of the importance of the detailed narratives that follow Dinah's story and since these all concern the success and prominence of Judah and Joseph, the very fact that there is a story about a woman, in the midst of these powerful stories about men, is structurally significant. It places her, at least externally, within a context of power as well. In a way it is surprising that Dinah's name is used in a rather familiar fashion and yet the story that follows is hardly about her. This is the first major story in Genesis that tells us more than something about Jacob/Israel's settlement in Canaan. In sum, the position of the tale, the events that it describes, and the woman that is clearly mentioned all combine to present an intriguing question about who Dinah was and why we do not hear her as we do all other significant women.

My basic assumption is that there was another story, more original, in which Dinah was a much more complex character, maybe even a heroine. Some of the evidence for an earlier original story (probably two layers of it) is in the very text that we have at our disposal. Since any oral tradition is powerful enough to compel those who transmit it to maintain as much of the original as possible, the redactors of the Dinah affair too were obliged to leave enough signals from the original sources to enable us partially to recover the "other" story of Dinah.

The first clue to a more original Dinah lies with "the Hivites," who are presented here as the main antagonists of the brothers (as well as of Dinah, who is said to have been raped by one of them). But there are at least two other significant peoples who are sometimes interchanged and confused with the Hivites.[6] The most important of them are the Hurrians, who were originally western Semitic and exceptionally expansive.[7] The Hurrians flourished in the Near East from the middle of the third to the end of the second millennium B.C.E. Their greatest political accomplishment was the Mitanni empire, centered in the mid-Euphrates Valley, in the vicinity of Harran (biblical Haran). The Hurrians borrowed extensively from the Mesopotamians and were well equipped to serve as instructors of the Hittites in writing, law, literature, religion, and art. Like other Mesopotamians, they did not practice circumcision. If the story of Dinah involves authentic Hivites, then why were they not circumcised? Circumcision had been practiced by Canaanite peoples, as it had been by Egyptians. We know that a Hurrian tribe was present in the eighteenth century and as late as the fourteenth century (the Amarna period) in the vicinity of Shechem. Did they encounter Hebrews there? In other words, did the tribes of Simeon and Levi settle that land? Or did they attempt to claim it from the Hurrians? The Genesis tradition insists that the Israelites' bought that portion of the land from Hamor and his "Hivite" clan: "And he [Jacob] bought the portion of the field where he has erected his tent from the sons of Hamor the father of Shechem, for one hundred qěśîṭâ. And he erected an altar there and called it El, the God of Israel" (33:19–20). Buying the land and erecting an altar were symbolic of control. But the redacted story of Dinah contradicts even that tradition by introducing the very violent encounter between the brothers and the "Hivites," in which the brothers were successful. Surely, though, this account at best is somewhat inflated, because we ultimately find out that these two tribes had no land of their own. How did they lose what they so "cleverly" fought for in the Dinah affair?

The second clue that might point to a different Dinah story is in 34:1, which tells us about Dinah's "going out to see the women of the land." This particular phraseology places Dinah within the framework of women and their activities, rather than men and their functions. Dinah's relatives and women ancestors are portrayed in the text as coming from Haran. In fact, the text presents all of the matriarchs as originating in Haran. In the story of Rebekah, for example, there are clear indications that women (at least while still in Haran) had a measure of power, and there was a special relationship between Rebekah and her mother. Certainly the text proclaims that Rebekah goes with Eliezer to join Isaac in his mother's tent out of her own free will. Even though the women of Genesis are not as powerful as the males, they do, at the very least, particpate in matters that have to do with their family and community. There is thus no question about these women's familiarity with Hurrian customs and social norms, since these people were very strongly present in Haran during the patriarchal period. In this framework, it is highly significant that Haran was an important center for moon worshipers. This Mesopotamian city had links with a goddess-worshiping community that indeed had special meaning for women. We know from the Amarna Letters that Hurrians worshiped Hepa, the mother goddess. Was Dinah exposed to that community before the family left Haran? Was it therefore natural for her to "go out" to see similar communities in Canaan as well? Or, an even more acute question: Was the Shechem community at the time of the initial telling of the story a community of Hurrians rather than Canaanites? Therefore, is there the possibility that Dinah's venture toward these "women" was a familiar one? One should not take lightly the classical commentaries on this particular verse which suggest that visiting with "the women of the land" was tantamount to worshiping in a Canaanite temple. Moreover, the usage of the noun *'ereṣ*, "land," is a sexual echo that brings to mind sexual rites practiced within the goddess cults. We have already seen that the classical prophets were enraged with the people who worshiped on every high hill and polluted the land with offerings to the Baal and Ashera (Jer 19:5; 32:29; Hos 2:10. Judg 8:33 actually uses the verb *zānâ*, "to prostitute," to describe Baal worship. References to prostitution abound in descriptions of worship of gods apart from Yahweh).

The third clue to Dinah's original function can be found in the use of the verb *ṭāmē'*, "to pollute." The narrative uses this particular word twice in describing Shechem's violation of Dinah. In the first instance, Jacob hears about that "pollution" (34:5), and in the second example the brothers react to the same information in a similar fashion (v. 13b). *Ṭum'â*, "pollution," is a profoundly religious concept dealt with extensively in the Priestly Code. It can refer to activities in all spheres of life but is used especially in the realm of temple worship and sex. Ezekiel, who is of a priestly family and prefers to use priestly and temple images in his prophetic oracles, describes at length men's "pollution" of other men's wives (18:11; 33:26), as well as the people's "pollution" of the temple (5:11). Ultimately, the removal of all "pollution" becomes the aspiration of the chosen community, who thus imitates Yahweh. Is it then possible that the use of this term once again points to Dinah's distinctive religious position? Was she attempting to continue in Canaan what she was used to in Haran? Or was she continuing something that her mother was involved with before moving to Canaan? Since it is difficult to determine her exact age (beyond the fact that she was a virgin), both possibilities must be taken into account. It is particularly poignant to emphasize the point about "pollution," because in the other biblical rape story (2 Samuel 13) associated with Dinah, this concept is not used by the narrator even though Tamar was also "tortured" by a prince, her half brother. In that story, even when Absalom undertakes the revenge in behalf of his sister, he refers to the fact of her "torture"-rape and not to her "pollution." I argued earlier in this study that on all counts the Amnon–Tamar rape incident is much more authentic than the Dinah "rape."

The fourth clue to a different Dinah story is in the word *zōnâ*, "prostitute," which is used only once in the text, when the brothers attempt to justify their destruction of the Hivite village. Although the Hebraic tradition uses this word to describe wayward women of all sorts, it is closely affiliated with *qĕdēšâ*, a holy prostitute. Curiously, the story of Judah and Tamar, which is textually so close to the story of Dinah (chap. 38), employs both terms interchangeably and presents Tamar in a semi-priestly environment hinting at the woman's priestly function, not just her familial concerns. The brothers' *zōnâ* characterization of Shechem's deed takes on a different dimension and, as in the other textual hints, points to their sister's possible involvement with cultic rituals not very different from those performed by Tamar, the Canaanite daughter-in-law of Judah, who is very highly praised.

Bearing all of these circumstances and linguistic issues in mind, there is now a real question about Shechem, who emerges from this analysis as possibly a Hurrian (not a Hivite) and who is said to have Dinah with him in his house (34:26b). Since structurally and linguistically it is difficult to accept his "rape" of Dinah (see the arguments throughout this book), the question is: What was she doing in his house? Possibly she was his legitimate wife. Since he is consistently described as a person of some stature in his community, his wife had stature too. More than that, Shechem is the only person in the tale that is sympathetic to Dinah. Even though the text describes him as a rapist first, it also depicts Shechem as a man in love.

Accounting for some of the irregularities in the text and placing it within a wider historical and cultural framework, it is plausible to view Dinah in a completely new light. She was not just an insignificant daughter who met with disaster early on in life. Neither was she a passive, submissive woman who was raped, crushed, and muted for the rest of her life. If indeed the initial story about her was based in Haran, and if her arrival in Shechem signified for her a kind of cultural continuity rather than a radical novelty, then she was different from the Dinah described (by the redactors) in Genesis.

As for the prominent role the brothers play in the Masoretic Text, it is possible to view it on two levels. The first level is purely political and advises us about the circumstances that brought about the territorial demise of the tribes of Simeon and Levi (particularly, Simeon). With or without the ruse that the redacted story uses, it seems that they have experienced a loss at the point of their contact with Shechem. On another level, it is plausible to maintain that the brothers who are described as particularly close to Dinah might have been in alliance with her or might have worked against her. We saw earlier that in the story of Rebekah and her family, there are brothers who are concerned about the well-being of their sister; they also are viewed as materially oriented and focused on their own economic improvement in the wake of their sister's marriage. In any case, for both the brothers and the sister, the point of no return was indeed in Shechem, the Canaanite/Hurrian center. Nonetheless, there is not too much more that can be said at this point about Dinah because there are no other words or gestures that might enable us to place her more concretely within an environment and landscape of power and authority.

NOTES

1. Who were the daughters of Jacob? One must assume that the various wives and concubines, especially those who were fertile, probably gave birth to a host of children, male and female. Because of the patriarchal slant

of the text, only the males are of any significance. By the same token, one should not lose sight of the fact that even some of the named males have very little impact on the events that occur in the text and that by and large there are only a few prominent men, who overshadow all the rest of the characters. The first patriarch, Abraham, is reported not to have had any daughters; neither did Isaac. Jacob seems to be blessed with women and children; consequently, the text seems to provide him and his wives with the opportunity of giving birth to female offspring. But there is no story, nor any other evidence, that these "daughters" were of any consequence. Finally, it should be noted that the same reference to "daughters" occurs later in the text, when Jacob and his family decide to "go down" to Egypt to reunite with Joseph and to escape the drought in Canaan (46:7). At that point, when the sons and their families are carefully enumerated, Dinah is mentioned too; as expected, she has no family of her own (v. 15).

2. In the majority of cases where the verb *dîn* is used, the subjects of justice are people on the fringes of society, e.g., "they did not judge orphans, justly" (Jer 5:28); or, "to avert justice from the poor" (Isa 10:2).

3. Isaac is preferred over Ishmael even though the text is explicit about Abraham's "love" for his firstborn. Jacob, the second born and Rebekah's favorite, secures the covenantal blessing.

4. See the story of the daughters of Zelophehad (Num 27:1-13), who inherited all of their father's wealth. Granted, the underlying assumption of the story is that, in the absence of sons, daughters were entitled to their father's possessions. However, this particular story has not been properly and fully studied yet.

5. It should be remembered that Leah is unlike the other matriarchs in the text in that she is not the patriarch's initial marital choice — probably because she is alluded to as "having soft eyes" (29:17), which in comparison with her sister (so the text maintains) meant that she was not beautiful. Neither is she initially barren. Nonetheless, she does have a voice in the text and is consulted (along with Rachel) by Jacob when the latter decides to leave the house of their father, Laban. Leah's tradition too has not been fully studied yet.

6. In the Amarna Letters (fourteenth century B.C.E.) the ruler of Jerusalem, a Jebusite center, is referred to as the "servant of Hepa," which is the Hurrian equivalent of the mother goddess. In the elaborate story of the census taken by David (2 Sam 24:16-25), there is an extended discussion and interchange between David and a person named Araunah. P. Kyle McCarter, Jr., points out that the name is not Semitic and that "it is often thought to be related to the Hurrian word *ibri* or *iwri*, 'lord, king'" (*II Samuel* [Anchor Bible 9; Garden City, NY: Doubleday, 1984]). McCarter goes on to conclude that since the chapter ends with David purchasing from

Araunah "the threshing floor" (v. 24) it is possible that he was "a pre-Israelite citizen of Jerusalem, a Jebusite of Hurrian or Hittite ancestry." The Hittite possibility is raised because of the textual expression of the "deal" struck between David and Araunah, which is reminiscent of the exchange between Abraham and "the Hittites" in Gen 23:3-16, where the patriarch negotiates for the cave of Machpelah in Hebron (McCarter, *II Samuel,* 512). See also my n. 4 in the Introduction (p. 19).

7. E. A. Speiser, "Hurrians," in *The Interpreter's Dictionary of the Bible* (New York: Abingdon, 1962); F. W. Bush, "Hurrians," in *The International Standard Bible Encyclopedia* (Grand Rapids: Eerdmans, 1982).

INDEXES

A. Index of Texts

B. Index of Names

Abraham (*cont.*)
  Ishmael's fate and, 76
  promise of a kingdom and, 19
  Shechem (the city) and, 117
Abram. *See* Abraham
Absalom, 26
  pollution and, 136
  violence of, 47
Achan, 126
Adam, 38-39
Aloni, Shulamit, 127
Amnon, 5
  lust and, 52
  midrashic view of, 89
  as rapist, 84-85
  violence against, 47
Aram. *See* Haran
Araunah, 138-139
Astarte, 52

Baal, 52
Begin, Menachem, 118-119
Ben Gurion, David, 114
Benjamin, 30
Biale, David, 26
Bilhah, 37
  love and, 61
Binur, Yoram, 121
Buber, Martin, 8-10
Buzia, Evetsam, 122

Cain, 10-11
  going out and, 81
Canaan, 12-15
  as Eden, 43-44
  move to, 22-23
Canaan (Ham's son), 35, 79
Canaanites
  in Genesis 34, 2
  goddess worship and, 113
  as strangers, 79

David, 5-6, 19
  court of, 24-26

David (*cont.*)
  promise of a kingdom and, 19
  Samuel and, 106
Dinah
  alienation and, 10
  birth of, 15-16
  as chattel, 108-109
  cleaving and, 86
  compared with Eve, 38-50
  courtship and, 67-69
  gender relations and, 54-56
  in Genesis 34, 1-4
  going out and, 59, 82, 93-94
  individual morality and,
    109-112
  as Leah's daughter, 82-85
  love and, 62-63
  lust and, 52
  midrashic view of, 89-91
  as rebel, 48-49
  role in family, 74-75
  silence and, 85-88, 115-116
  strangers and, 80-81
  in the tent, 70-73
  torture and, 113
  transition and, 58
  unredacted, 130-137
  violence against, 45-47
  weakness of, 103

Eden, 38-41
Egyptians, 113
Eli, 106-107
Eliezer, 32
  courtship and, 63-64
  going out and, 58
Elohim. *See* God; Yahweh
Er, 14, 21
Esau, 15-16, 64
  contrast with Jacob, 66
  inheritance and, 30
Eve, 38-50
  as rebel, 48-49
  violence against, 45-46

C. Index of Subjects

DATE DUE